It's NOT a Cookie

So STOP Giving it Away!

A Guide to Adolescent Relationships

SANDRA J. DIXON

*Priority*ONE
publications

Detroit, Michigan USA

*Priority*ONE Publications
P. O. Box 361332 | Grosse Pointe, MI 48236
E-mail: info@priorityonebooks.com
URL: http://www.priorityonebooks.com

ISBN: 978-1-933972-72-5 – Print
ISBN: 978-1-933972-73-2 – eBook

Editing by Patricia Hicks
Cover and Interior design by Christina Dixon

Printed in the United States of America

DEDICATION

To my daughter Alexis and nieces Jaaucklyn and Lauryn.
Even as you are growing into adulthood, please remember that
you are fearfully and wonderfully made. You are beautiful young
ladies, inside and out. Continue to trust God and He will give you
your heart's desires.

And to my GRADS Mommies,
I am grateful to have been a part of guiding you through your
pregnancy and parenting journey, one of God's most precious
gifts. You'll never know how much I learned through you.

CONTENTS

ACKNOWLEDGMENTS

Writing this book has been a journey! The one person who has prodded me along this journey has been my coach, mentor and friend, Christina Dixon. Thank you so much for pushing me to finish. I have always believed so strongly in the message of the book and when I felt like I just wasn't going to get it done, you came alongside and encouraged me. I am most grateful.

We live in a world where many girls grow up without having meaningful relationships with their fathers. Some have never felt that love or have an idea of what that is like. I reached out to several fathers to ask them to write letters to the daughters that will be reading this book but to write based on their own experience. These were fathers of all ages, with daughters of all ages. They are not "perfect" fathers with "perfect" daughters. The common thread in all these letters is that "you are loved." The most important relationship we can have is with our heavenly Father. When you read these heartfelt letters, I believe that these are messages that were ordained and penned by God for your situation. I thank all the fathers that contributed:

Joshua Luton, Gary Morton, Jacques Smith, Sr., Bishop Emery Lindsay, my nephew Geoffrey Golden, my brother Dr. Leonard N. Moore. Special mention to Dr. Brian Hayes, who wrote the letter before succumbing to cancer. May his daughters always feel his love and presence.

Chapter One:
My Story

When I was in third grade, I was a Brownie Girl Scout and we had meetings on Tuesdays after school. We wore our little brown uniforms with an orange sash. Each week, one girl was designated to bring the snack for the next week. If it was your turn, you took the orange bucket home and brought it back with the snack inside. This week it was my friend's turn to bring the treat. Her name was Lori. Back when I was a young girl, Oreo cookies were a really big deal. My mother never bought us name brand snacks. As a matter of fact, she seldom bought us snacks at all. Lori's mother sent Oreo cookies for the snack. Lori and I both had a crush on a boy in the 6th grade, whose name was Craig. Of course, he didn't like us because we were only in third grade. He probably wouldn't have even known we existed if my sister wasn't his classmate. Every day when we would see him on the playground, we would ask him, "Craig, do you like us?" Of course, his response was always "no" but this particular day he saw the Oreo cookies in the bucket. He said, "If you give me a pack of Oreo cookies, I will like you." Since she had two packs, I begged her to give him one of the packs. She finally agreed. The next day we saw him on the playground and again we asked the question, "Do you like us?" His reply was, "If you bring me Oreo cookies every day, I will like you." I got excited. This was easy, I thought. The only problem, of course, was my mother didn't buy Oreo cookies. Luckily, Lori had more sense than me and said that we wouldn't be bringing him cookies and that was the end of that. I often laugh when I think back about that whole situation. However, as I observe adolescents in relationships today, all too often the cookie has been replaced and it's not so funny. The "Craig's" in life are saying, "If you give me what I want, I will like you" and there aren't enough "Lori's" around to tell the "Sandra's" that this is not okay.

For most of my adult life, I have worked with teens in various capacities. I have taught middle school, high school; and have worked with church youth groups on the local and national levels. My most memorable experiences were when I taught an in-school Teen Parent program at two different schools in the Cleveland, OH area. One suburban, one inner-city. My conclusion from all these experiences is the same; teens are often unaware of the Physical, Social and Emotional consequences of being in pre-marital sexual relationships; and the consequences are the same for all teens regardless of race, socio-economic status, age or religious affiliations. This book will include quotes and stories that I have gathered from teens over the years. At the end of each chapter is a "Dear Daughter" letter. These are letters written by real fathers to you. The inspiration was their own daughters. Your father may not be in your life, but these fathers wanted to share a natural father's love with you just as our heavenly father loves you. My prayer and hope that after you read this book you will have the tools to have a healthy relationship and to realize that "it's not an Oreo cookie" so please don't give it away.

Chapter Two
"What's Love Got to Do with It?"

Three things will last forever—faith, hope, and love—
and the greatest of these is love." I Cor. 13:13

*"I know that Ken loves me. Ken loves me, and I love him. I don't have to
worry about using any condom, because I know that he is not messing around
with anyone but me. I don't care what you say, I love him, and you can't tell
me what he is or isn't doing, because you don't know him like I do."*

(Sheri, age 18, 5mos. pregnant)

*"He is going to always take care of little Brad. I don't have to get child
support because I love him. and he loves me. We've been together for 3 years.
After we graduate, we're going to get married. I'm sick and tired of hearing
about child support because I'll never take him to child support because we
love each other, and he takes care of his baby."*

(Kayla, age 17, little Brad, 7 months)

*"I really love Raymond. He doesn't have any kids and he wants me to have a
baby. I want to have his baby because we're going to get married anyway."
"But you're only 16, he's 23; you're still in school and have your whole future
to worry about." "I know, but he doesn't have any kids and wants me to have
one, and I want to have one."*

(Cynthia, age 16, pre-pregnant)

We'll hear more about these girls in later chapters.

LOVE, LOVE, LOVE. "I love him; he loves me." In our society there is no way of getting around it. Love is everywhere. Whenever you turn on the radio you hear love songs. It doesn't matter what kind of music it is, it could be slow ballads, jazz songs, rap songs, soft rock, country and everything in between. Our TV shows and movies are dominated by themes of "Love". Billboards and advertising are selling "love." Let me pause here. I think I've made a mistake. I keep using the word "love" and I should be using the word "lust". Let me start again. **LUST, LUST, and LUST.** "I lust for him; he lusts for me." In our society there is no way of getting around it. Lust is everywhere. Whenever you turn on the radio you hear songs about lust. It doesn't matter what kind of music it is, it could be slow songs, jazz songs, rap music, soft rock, country and everything in between. Lust is streaming 24/7. Think about the most popular TV shows that young people watch? What are they about? She (or he) is sleeping with one person this week and then next week she (or he) is with somebody else. Women fighting over men. Men fighting over men. All kinds of sin. Seldom do you see healthy, strong marriages and relationships portrayed. Even the church folks are setting their DVR's, so they don't miss these shows. Many of the commercials that we see are selling lust. Sometimes we can't even tell what product is actually being promoted. Billboards and advertising are selling lust. I think that's a bit more accurate. As easy as it is for society to get the two confused, imagine how difficult it must be for you to understand the concept. If you are currently in a relationship, I want you to think about your relationship. Maybe you're not in a relationship right now, so think about the last time that you were in a relationship. Did your eyes light up when he walked into the room? Did you think about him so much that you couldn't eat when he

4

wasn't around? Did you sit in class and daydream about him so much so that you couldn't get your work done? Were you ready to fight anyone that you felt was interfering with your relationship? Did you have to be with him 24/7? Did you call him just to see if he was home? Did you ride by his job when he said he had to work late? Did you get upset when he did not immediately return your text? Did you have sex with him after only knowing him for a short time? Did he tell you that he loved you after a few days, or even weeks or months? Did he tell you that he loved you and couldn't see himself without you after knowing you for only a couple of weeks? If this describes your relationship, then let me bring the bad news; it's not love; it is, or was, just "LUST". So just what is lust? I am so glad you asked. Lust is an intense craving or desire to have something or someone. Lust and infatuation are similar in that you're living in fantasy land with no regard to reality. So, what's the difference between love and lust? Look at you, asking all these good questions. I have an answer. Why don't you take a look at the table on the next page and hopefully you will see the difference.

A Relationship Based on Love Means...	A Relationship Based on Infatuation Means...
Knowing the person well	*Love at first sight*
Loving the whole person	*Being obsessed with one characteristic*
Experiencing feelings of self-confidence and security	*Feelings of guilt, insecurity, and frequent frustration*
Pleasant feelings toward other people	*Usually being self-centered and restricted*
Many shared interests and an ongoing sense of being alive together	*Frequent boredom, especially when there is no sexual excitement or amusement*
Changes and growth in the relationship; developing and deepening feelings	*Little change in the relationship over time*
Reasonable and attainable daydreams	*Unreasonable daydreams*
Physical attraction is a relatively small part	*Physical attraction is a big part*
Physical expression of affection begins later	*Physical expression of affection starts right away*
An enduring relatively stable relationship	*Sudden changes in the relationship for no reason*

If you looked at the right side of the chart and said, "That sounds like me," just know that you are not alone. Unfortunately, many of you will find yourselves in these unhealthy relationships and won't know what to do. I want to make sure you have it clear. Think about it this way; Lust is like a "Stir-Fry"; it cooks in very high heat, very fast; it sizzles, and it's very tasty, but it takes a lot to fill you up. Love on the other hand is like a Pot Roast, it's best when it has marinated for a while, then placed in a slow cooker, with low heat, cooking in its own juices for hours; but when it's ready, it's tender, it's delectable, it's filling and, most importantly, it's satisfying. Delectable, filling and satisfying, doesn't that sound delish!

Love is like a pot roast...

Lust is like a stir fry!

Latrice was a student who was entering her final month of pregnancy. It was January, and she was sharing with the class how she had spent her New Year's Eve. She found out that her "boyfriend" was going out partying on New Year's Eve, but he wasn't going to take her. That was probably a good decision, seeing how she was due at any time. She thought that she wasn't invited because he was going to be out with another female. She told the class that she had talked her cousin into driving her around from place to place looking for him. I asked her what she planned to do if she had found him. She said that she didn't know what she was going to do, but she was determined to find him. Here I was trying

7

to picture this 16-year-old girl with her belly sticking way out, riding around from place to place looking for her man. Luckily, she didn't find him. Lust can make people act irrationally. Relationships that are not based on mutual trust and commitment most often lead to discontentment and the inability to provide satisfaction. Add a baby to this equation, and you have the recipe for disaster.

EBONY was a 17-year-old young woman who had limited social experiences. She found herself caught up in the drama of a sweet-talking older guy. Since she had been "looking for love," it was easy for her to become infatuated with Ray when he showed her a little attention. Ebony was so starved for attention that Ray was easily able to find his way into her heart and into her panties. That is how the cycle of destruction started. Ebony soon found herself cutting school to be with him. She began lying to her mother, her friends, and others about her whereabouts. Even after her friends advised her to end the relationship, she insisted on keeping it going. She soon found out that her "Bae" was expecting a baby by another woman. You would have thought that would have been enough for her to end the relationship. Nope. This did not slow her down one bit. Of course, the lies would follow. He would tell her things like "Me and my baby's mama aren't even together anymore." "I don't even know if it's my baby." "I care about you and only want to be with you." I don't even have to tell you how that played out. In the words of Lauren Lake, *"Ray, it has been determined that you* **are** *the father."* So now here Ray was, a young father in denial, but Ebony was still determined to keep a relationship going with him. This led to altercations between Ebony and Ray's "Baby Mama," but Ebony was still so infatuated by him that she could not let him go. He was so flattered by the attention that he would not let her go either. He thought he was "the man." I bet he was thinking, "I got a newborn, and this girl is still sweatin' me." In Ebony's mind there was only one option that anyone in her situation would choose; become pregnant herself. "That'll show him – I'll keep him in my life forever." Let's fast forward a few months. There she was pregnant and alone. On top of that, she had dropped out of college, and her mother didn't even know. I wish I could say that there was a happy ending. Unfortunately, there was a precious, innocent baby girl who was caught in the middle of all this drama.

Lust can make you do dumb things. The society that we live in makes it hard for young people to get around it. Many of the TV shows that we watch glamorize lustful relationships. What we really see is fantasy relationships. Boy meets girl, falls in love with girl, proposes and marries girl all within the 30 minutes. Or they might not even  get married. They fall in love, move in with each other after one or two dates. It's what I call the Hallmark movie syndrome. We are all suckers for a happy, mushy ending. Even though the outcomes are so predictable, we still can't get enough of them. When we look at them, our hearts flutter as we see another happy relationship on the books. Reality check girls: This is TV! What we don't see is that two weeks later the girl finds out that the boy has given her an STD because he has been cheating on her with his ex-girlfriend. We don't see that the boy has left the girl pregnant and alone. We don't even see the girl changing her mind, after realizing that she didn't really love the boy. The closest that we come to reality is on the "real-life courtroom" shows which seem to be over occupied with conducting paternity tests for women who have been behaving recklessly. Sadly, we find that entertaining. What is wrong with our values as a society where we parade ignorant females on national TV, who obviously have had sex with multiple men within a short period of time, to help them try to sort out the "baby-daddy" mystery? I also wonder about the values of the women themselves who seem to show no shame by their should-be embarrassing situation. Guess what? Regardless of what you've been told, you can learn from other's mistakes. You can look at these situations and determine that you don't want your life to be like that.

The people that seem to be idolized in our society, unfortunately, cannot be looked upon to provide examples of positive, healthy relationships. Reality shows such as Love and Hip Hop, Basketball Wives, Real Housewives of any city, and Marriage at First Sight, are just a few shows that people watch but they don't portray healthy, godly relationships. We are forced to hear about some of our sports and entertainment superstars as they have babies with different partners time and time again.. This is often headline news, as if it's a good thing. What message are we getting? That it's okay since everybody's doing it? God's standards don't matter anymore? It is so sad that there are very few, if any, good examples for you to see. Hebrews 13:8 says, *"Jesus Christ is the same yesterday and today and forever."* That means that we must keep the word of God close. It is easy to get the message confused if we stay focused on what's on TV, the internet and on social media. Please, please don't look at the world's examples to define the standard for you.

If you really want to know what love is, look to the author of love. There are, on average, 400 references to love in the Bible. God, the Father, is the author of love so we can always find the real deal about love. In Chapter 13 of I Corinthians, the "love chapter", we find the biblical characteristics of love and many of these directly contradict the characteristics of many adolescent relationships we see today.

never gives up
cares more for others than for self
doesn't want what it doesn't have
doesn't strut
doesn't have a swelled head
doesn't force itself on others
doesn't fly off the handle
isn't always "me first"
doesn't keep score of the sins of others
doesn't revel when others grovel
takes pleasure in flowering of truth
puts up with anything
trusts God always
always looks for the best
never looks back, but keeps going to the end
never dies

There are three that remain- faith, hope and love- and the greatest of these is LoVE

Scripture taken from 1 Corinthians 13:4-8 MSG and verse 13 TLB

You may be thinking, "Really? This is love?" Yep, it sure is!

The rest of this book is designed to help clarify what love really is and what love really isn't. It can be difficult going through this time in your life where love has been watered down. As you read, ask God to give you a greater understanding of relationships and how he has designed them to work.

Prayer for Me

Dear God,
It's me _____.
Thank you for being a God that cares about me and loves me. Please let me know the truth about love and relationships. I want to honor you with my whole heart, my mind and my body. I have mistaken infatuation for love. I have listened to my friends and the media teach me about relationships. Open my eyes and my ears that I will see and hear your truth. Open my heart so that I may receive it. I love you and want to live a life that you will be proud of. Thank you for loving me.
                          In Jesus' Name. Amen.

Dear Daughter,

You are amazing! When I look at you, I'm filled with gratefulness that God trusted me enough to be your father. I want you to know that you are one of a kind. You are special! This world and my world is a better place because you're in it. So I want you to live out the fullness of your potential. I want you to be your best self! I want you to realize every dream that God had about you when He made you.

Princess, you're going to experience a lot of things in life that will try to steal your light. Situations will come and will tempt you to live in fear, anxiety, low self-esteem, depression, and despair. But you don't have to give in to those feelings, daughter. The feelings will come, yes, but they don't have to define your life. Instead, you can live in joy, peace, courage, and confidence! In order to live like this and to fulfill your purpose, I ask you to always be humble, helpful, and hopeful.

Being humble means that you don't think of yourself above anyone else. It means that you remain teachable and that you always remember that you need God and other people. Being helpful means that you do your best to encourage, empower, and assist others so they can be all God has called them to be. There may be some moments or days when you feel like the only way to make it is to only help yourself, but the opposite is true! If you help others to be their best, I believe that God will always give you the help you need to be your best. Being hopeful means that you live looking UP! No matter what you go through, princess, remember that God sits on the throne and that He will use even the worst situations to work for your good. No matter how many times situations in life knock you down, always let God pick you back up. And no matter how many mistakes you make, know that failure is not final! Life won't always be easy, but God will carry you through! Stay fierce, princess! Don't let the world water you down. Always look to Jesus and never give in to fear. I'm so proud of who you are and who you are becoming. I will leave you with words my uncle used to always say to our family: "I love you. I'm praying for you every day. Be blessed and be a blessing!"

Love,
Your Dad

Chapter Three:
The Souvenir

For my loins are filled with a loathsome disease:
And there is no soundness in my flesh. Psalm 38:7 (KJV)

I don't know about you, but I love to travel. There was a time that when Friday came, I had to be in the car or in the air going somewhere. I never liked to stay at home. Even now I'd rather save up my money to take a trip than spend it on most other things. Before I became a parent, I had three nephews that lived in town. If I went on a trip, I always had to bring them back a souvenir. They didn't even ask me how my trip was; it was just, "what did you bring us back?" So everywhere I went, I found myself looking for the street vendors who were selling the 3 for $10 t-shirts, or the $1 key chains or the souvenir mugs. It didn't matter to them what it was, I just knew that I'd better not come home empty-handed. We all like souvenirs! It shows that we were thought of when a loved one was away, or it was a reminder of something special.

Once, before I got married, I was out of town with a girlfriend and my boyfriend was out of town at the same time in a different city. I was in the mall looking for something to buy him, and my friend asked me why I was buying him something. I told her that I had to buy him something because I expected him to bring me back something. She didn't understand why we would buy each other souvenirs from cities that we each had been to. I couldn't really explain it to her, except that it showed we were both thinking about each other while we were apart, and we like to get gifts; okay so we were a little shallow too.

In relationships, you do things like this. You might go to an amusement park and buy the pictures or videos from the rides for a souvenir. You might save ticket stubs from events that you went to together. You take plenty of pictures and post for all the world to see. People take selfies with celebrities after shows. Some people, although I don't recommend this, tattoo each other's names on their bodies.

Tattoos are permanent. If you're a teenager, there's no way that your parent should allow you to get a tattoo of your current boyfriend's name. Sure, there is a very expensive procedure that can remove tattoos, but it is so much easier to not do it in the first place. If you're thinking of doing this, immediately turn to the Chapter entitled "Slow Down, Adulthood Loading." These types of souvenirs, for the most part, are harmless memoirs of the relationship. If you're not careful though, you can have other not-so-harmless souvenirs. I want you to do some fast-forward thinking with me for a few minutes.

I want you to imagine that you are about 25 years old. You have met the man of your dreams. He is tall, dark and handsome; everything you always wanted in a man. He says that you are everything he has ever wanted in a woman. These are his words: "Let me tell you about the love of my life; She is fine; she has a body that is fire! Her hair is gorgeous; her smile, captivating and she is as beautiful on the inside as she is on the outside. I've waited all my life for her. I have saved my body just for her like God told me to and I am now ready for everything that God has promised me in this marriage." As many couples, the bride and groom exchange gifts. You decide to exchange your gifts the night before the wedding as you spend your final few moments alone, as boyfriend and girlfriend before you become husband and wife. He has saved up to buy you a beautiful diamond pendant that will accentuate the neckline on your wedding gown just so, and he's getting goosebumps just thinking about how he'll feel when he watches you cascade down the aisle. There you are, sitting on the swing on your back porch where you sat when he proposed, while the gentle June breeze is ever so slight. You say, "You go first." He says, "Sweetheart, I love you more that life itself. I don't know what I'll ever do without you. You are the icing on my cake, the cream cheese on my bagel, the toppings on my pizza and the missing rib in my side." (All right, I know that's a little corny.) He then reaches into his pocket and pulls out this beautiful diamond pendant and watches as your eyes light up and a tear begins to fall gently down your cheek. He reaches over and wipes it from your face. You sit there, stunned, not knowing what to say. He tells you to say nothing because your expression says it all. It's your turn. You reach into your purse and pull out a beautiful gold watch with diamond accents. It is gorgeous. You put it on his wrist, and he is floating on air! You say, "This isn't all I have to give." You begin, "When I was 15, I met this dude named Carlos. I really liked Carlos. We dated for a few weeks, and I had sex with him. I found out later that I had Chlamydia. I got it treated but the doctor told me that there would be a 25% chance that I wouldn't be able to have children. Then, when I was 17, I met David. David and I talked about getting married because I really loved him. He was 23 at the time. I got pregnant and he left me. I knew I couldn't raise a baby on my own, so I had an abortion. It was at that time I found out that I had Chlamydia again. This time it had advanced to PID (Pelvic inflammatory disease) which can lead to cervical cancer. I've been getting treatments, but now there's a 50% chance that I may not be able to have children. I hope this doesn't change the way you feel about me, because ever since I met you, my life has changed. I was much younger then, and I know I made some bad decisions, but since I've become an adult, I've gotten myself together and all I can do is think about being your wife."

I know what you're probably thinking; "this is unrealistic, and it won't happen to me." Well, think again. I want you to know that there's a young lady who may very well one day be having this conversation. Darla is a beautiful young lady inside and out. Unfortunately, this story is her story. Past relationships, like Darla's, have left many teenagers with souvenirs that they really didn't need in a relationship, nor did they ever expect to get at the beginning.

Let's take a look at some of these unwanted souvenirs. Check this out:

Today in America 8219 teenagers will contract a sexually transmitted infection; almost 3000 will become pregnant; about 1600 will give birth to a baby and tomorrow it will start over again, and the next day, and the next day. This chapter deals specifically with sexually transmitted infections (STIs), and we'll talk about adolescent parenting later.

Whenever I teach about STIs, students are usually "spooked" out of having sex for a few days. Unfortunately, like everything else, the fear quickly fades back into reckless behavior.

In the 1970's there were only about five identified sexually transmitted diseases. Today, there are more than 20 identified sexually transmitted diseases or infections that are plaguing America. Teenagers are contracting diseases in record numbers. The reasons for this include, but are not limited to, the fact that

18

young people have become sexually active earlier, and are marrying later; many teens, especially females, are having sex with older partners; and teenagers are less likely than older women to use contraception. Can you guess which group has the highest numbers of chlamydia? Since this book is for teen girls you might have guessed it; young women aged 15-24. This group has nearly 62% of all cases of chlamydia. Wow! The scary part of this whole epidemic is that most teens that are affected don't even know it. Most teens believe that if they have sex tonight and wake up tomorrow feeling fine, without any visible signs of disease on their face or body, they are okay; so they never get tested for diseases.

There was a movie I was watching once, based on true events, where a lot of girls in the same school were contracting syphilis. When they identified the young man that was responsible for starting the epidemic, he was called into the school health clinic. When the nurse told him what they had discovered, his response was "just give me my magic bullet and I'll be on my way." In other words, he didn't 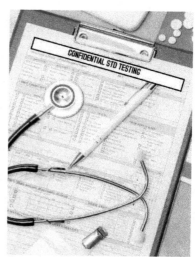 care at all that he was spreading syphilis. He showed no remorse or any signs of regret. He just wanted the antibiotic. This was not his first time going through the process and probably wouldn't be his last. His attitude is probably like a lot of teen guys. Can you imagine if you had been one of the girls? What a tragedy.

Adolescents ages 15-24 account for nearly half of the 20 million new cases of STIs each year. Today, four in 10 sexually active teen girls have had an STI that can cause infertility and even death. As if this isn't bad enough, African American teenage girls are the most severely affected. The Centers for Disease Control, the CDC, conducted a study and found that nearly half of all sexually active young African American women (48 percent) were infected with an STI, compared to 20 percent of young white women. Overall, African Americans (male and female) lead the pack in incidences of Gonorrhea, Syphilis, Chlamydia and HIV/AIDS. STIs are not only scary, but they can mess up your reproductive system, can stop you from becoming pregnant, can cause cancer and can even cost you your life!

I don't know what else I can say to you to make you see that this is a very serious matter that we are dealing with. I can guarantee that you probably know someone who has at least one STI. If you are sexually active, that person could very well be you. I'm going to say this now and you will continue to hear this throughout this book; this does not have to be you!! God has a plan for your life that is so much greater than this. *Jeremiah 29:11 says this, "For I know the plans I have for you, says the Lord. They are plans for good and not for disaster, to give you a future and a hope."* This is to remind you that God is concerned about you. He has plans for you. He knows your past, your present and your future. Just trust him!

In case you are not really sure about this whole STI thing, I am going to share some information about them. Sexually transmitted infections fall into two categories, viral and bacterial.

SEXUALLY TRANSMITTED INFECTIONS

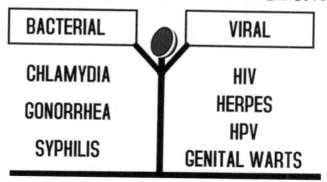

BACTERIAL	VIRAL
CHLAMYDIA	HIV
GONORRHEA	HERPES
	HPV
SYPHILIS	GENITAL WARTS

The viral infections, if contracted, you will have them for life. The bacterial infections can be treated, but only if you know that you've been infected. The viral infections include herpes, HPV, genital warts, and HIV. The bacterial infections include Chlamydia, Gonorrhea and Syphilis. It is important to understand some of these key points about all STIs in America today: STIs are not discriminatory. These diseases may be spread through vaginal, anal and oral sex. Females are more likely than males to get infected. Condoms are not guaranteed protection against STIs. In case you have never heard of some of the STIs that have been mentioned; I'm going to give you some of the highlights about STIs.

AIDS (Acquired Immune Deficiency Syndrome)

- The deadliest of them all. It is caused by the human immunodeficiency virus (HIV).
- It kills the immune system, allowing many dangerous diseases to take over.
- No cure! It is fatal.

GENITAL HERPES
- A virus that causes a burning, tingling or itching feeling, followed by painful blister-like bumps on the sex organs.
- After the sores heal, the virus hides in the nerve cells and can reactivate one to six times per year.
- If untreated and passed on to a newborn, the disease can cause mental retardation or death.
- Can be controlled, but there is no cure.
- Don't be tricked by the commercials for the medicine, you will be on this medicine every day for the rest of your life.

GENITAL WARTS
- Can develop on the sex organs of both the male and the female.
- Can also appear on and around the rectum.
- Warts are small, with a pink or red appearance, and are usually bunched together.
- Can be burned or frozen off but can return.

CHLAMYDIA
- The leading infection among teens.
- More common among teens than among older men and women.
- No early symptoms, but early detection is important.
- The main cause of Pelvic Inflammatory Disease (PID) in women which can lead to ectopic (tubal) pregnancies and sterility.
- Can be cured if detected.

GONORRHEA
- Teens have higher rates of gonorrhea than do sexually

active men and women aged 20-44.

- In men this germ infects the urinary tract, causing painful urination and a discharge of yellow-greenish pus from the urethra coming out through the penis.
- Most women show no symptoms, so you **must** get tested.
- A major cause of pelvic inflammatory disease (PID) and ectopic pregnancies (that's when the baby is growing in the fallopian tubes) in women and sterility in men.
- Is treatable with antibiotics, although some strains are resistant to it.

SYPHILIS

- The small, reddish sores of an early syphilis infection usually go unnoticed.
- This is followed by a body rash, which indicates a worsening infection.
- Can seriously damage the heart, brain and other organs.
- Can be treated and cured with antibiotics, but any damage that was previously done cannot be reversed.

Other diseases that may be sexually transmitted include trichomoniasis, bacterial vaginosis, scabies and pubic lice. You can look those up on your own. So, you see, catching any of these can mess you up!

Trying to stay pure and not sin seems like a very difficult, if not impossible, task. Some teens probably even wonder why anyone would want to stay pure. Sometimes, it might really seem unpopular to not have sex. It is probably even more unpopular to walk around with a disease in your body. Although not wanting to get a disease is a great deterrent, as a Christian, there is a greater deterrent. When we accept Christ as our Savior, we take on His characteristics. We become citizens of heaven and must represent the standards that Christ represents. God wants us to be like Jesus. The only way that we can be like Jesus is to allow God to transform our lives, our hearts and our minds to be like him. If we are Christians, there are rights and there are responsibilities to being a Christian. One of those responsibilities is keeping your temple clean, that is your body. *"Don't you realize that your body is the temple of the Holy Spirit, who lives in you and was given to you by God? You do not belong to yourself, for God bought you with a high price. So, you must honor God with your body"* (I Corinthians 6:19-20). If you don't do things God's way, you are opening yourself up to getting any one of these souvenirs.

There are many of you who are reading this book and are thinking that only dirty or careless girls and guys contract sexually transmitted diseases. In discussion groups that I have had with young men, I hear comments like, "you can look at a girl and tell if she's got something" or "she's clean, she's not like them hoes out there." Young ladies unfortunately feel the same way. Somehow, they believe that if a guy is physically attractive, then he must not be carrying any harmful disease. I even had a student tell me that her mother told her that before she had sex she should look and touch to see if her partner had a disease. DON'T BE FOOLED! Sexually transmitted diseases are equal opportunity attackers. They don't care what you look like. They don't care if you only buy name brand clothes and shoes. They don't care what sport you play. They don't care if you get all A's or all F's in your classes. They don't care about how many IG followers you have, or how many views you got on your TikTok video. Sexually transmitted diseases don't discriminate at all! They often strike without warning. If you have sex outside of the boundaries in which God created sex to be enjoyed, you are at risk for contracting a disease. Let me repeat that; if you have sex outside of the boundaries in which God created and intended sex to be enjoyed in, you are at risk for contracting a disease and at risk for all the emotional and social consequences that go along with that decision. Another lie out there is that if you are in a serious relationship, then you don't have to worry about catching a disease. Well, that is true if one of two conditions exist. One, if that relationship does not include any sexual activity, and two, if that relationship is a committed marriage. Outside of this, you are putting yourself at risk. At the beginning of the book, I introduced some young people. I want to tell you more about Sheri. I met her when she was three months pregnant. She insisted that she would continue to have unprotected sex with her "baby's daddy" because she could trust him. There was nothing that I could say that would convince her otherwise. As a matter of fact, she

If you have sex outside of the boundaries in which God created sex to be enjoyed, you are at risk for catching a disease.

actually had an attitude with me because I suggested that she didn't know for sure what Ken was doing when he wasn't around her, and for the sake of herself and the baby, she might want to think twice about what she was doing. Well, I'm going to take you to the end of the story. By the end of the school year, Ken was in jail for domestic violence against Sheri. During that year, she had domestic violence charges on her also. Sheri had contracted three different sexually transmitted infections from Ken and was awaiting test results which would determine how far her diseases had advanced. I don't know what the outcomes of these tests were. I only know that for the rest of her life she will be living with disease in her body, whether it lies dormant or becomes active at some point. She has a beautiful baby daughter who will always be a reminder of this relationship. By now you're probably wondering; "where are the stories with the happy endings? I know 'this and that' can happen to you, but everyone doesn't turn out this bad." The Bible says in Romans 6:23 NIV that the *"wages of sin is death."* It also says in Galatians 6:7 *"Don't be misled — you cannot mock the justice of God. You will always harvest what you plant."* In other words, your actions have consequences. The books of the Old Testament remind us time and time again of the consequences of disobedience to God. Nothing's changed. There are many blessings for those who obey God. There is peace, contentment and satisfaction that come from doing things God's way. As a teenager, you are faced with many, many opportunities to do the wrong thing. It is so easy to go along with the crowd and do what you think everybody else is doing. That is what the enemy wants you to do. The enemy is Satan. He is real. There are some people that think that the devil is not real. Well, let me tell you that he is not only real, but he doesn't need sleep either so his full-time job, 24/7 is looking for people to take down. He is destroying young people in record numbers. The devil is good at what he does. He is a marketing genius. If you know anything about advertising, the goal is to get you, the consumer, to purchase goods and services based on the information that you see or hear. Recently, I was watching TV and saw the commercial for this barbecue bacon cheeseburger topped with pulled pork. It looked so good! I couldn't wait to get to this restaurant to try it. When I finally got there, of course the burger didn't look like the commercial, and it didn't taste as good as it looked. What a letdown. There was a girl who had ordered a custom designed prom dress online. She sent in her measurements, picked out the fabric and when she finally got it a couple of days before prom, it looked nothing like she thought it would, besides that, the colors were wrong and it didn't fit. She was so mad that she almost didn't even go to prom. Her mother made her go to the store, pick out a dress and go anyway. Well, Satan is no different. Would he actually tell you the truth? Would he say to you, "Latanya, look at Damon over there, ain't he fine? You know he's the captain of the football team and works out every day. I see him looking at you, but I think you should know that he has a reputation for trying to get girls in bed. He knows that your dad is the minister at the biggest church in town, and he sees you as a challenge. He bet his buddies that he could get in your pants. Latanya run the other way. He's not for you." Nice - but I don't think so. It would probably be more like this, "Latanya, look at Damon over there checking you out. I noticed that he's been looking at you a lot lately. Look at his body. Do you see that "six-pack?" He works out every day. All the girls like him, but he's feeling you. Just think of what everyone will say when they find out that you are going out with Damon. He could have any girl he wants, but he wants you. Don't blow this one, Latanya. You may never have this opportunity again." "You lyin' and you know you lyin." That's just what we need to tell the devil! He is the author of confusion and the "father of lies" according to John 8:44. As a matter of fact it also says, *"there is no truth in him."* If ever there was a world of confusion, it is now. There is no other way to truth and life than through Jesus Christ who himself said *"I am the way, the truth and the life"* John 14:6

By now you're wondering, "What can I do to prevent STIs?" There is one definite, sure way to prevent yourself from ever getting infected by any of the sexually transmitted diseases; that is to remain sexually pure until marriage. Time and time again you will realize that God's way is the best way for all areas of our life. Some of your peers may laugh at you when they find out that you're a virgin. Some of the ones laughing are probably virgins themselves, and the others probably wish that they were. We were discussing STIs in my Child Development class. There were a few girls in the class who had been very vocal about being sexually active. When we talked about getting tested for STIs, a couple of the girls talked about how nervous they would get awaiting test results for STIs. They then went on to say that they would get tested regularly. They were surprised to learn that condoms don't provide protection from all diseases and that many of the infections don't have symptoms. That's part of the "safe-sex" lie. Maybe you've already messed up,

28

taken the plunge and haven't waited for the committed, monogamous relationship of marriage. Guess what? You can stop now! Yeah, I said it; you can stop now. You can make the decision from this day forward to stop having sex until marriage. Just because you have said "Yes" in the past does not mean you can't say "No" from now on. So, the question now is, just what is sex? If I just stop having intercourse, is everything else okay? Let me tell you a little something about these diseases. They can live outside of the genital area and can enter through open sores even if you never, ever have intercourse. Think about when you were a little girl and they taught you about "good touch, bad touch." Nobody should come in direct contact with any part that should be covered up by a swimming suit. That's male **and** female swimwear. I said *should* because some swimming suits don't cover up anything, but I think you understand. This may mean a drastic change in the relationship that you are in now. This may even mean ending your current relationship. You must be firm. I listen to guys talk, and they really do think that if you've said yes before, then they automatically have a free pass. Maybe you feel that way too. Again, let's think about who's planting those lies in your head. God is true to His promise. He will help you get out of any relationship that is not pleasing to him, if you ask. *"And now to him who can keep you on your feet, standing tall in His bright presence, fresh and celebrating—to our one God, our only Savior, through Jesus Christ, our Master, be glory, majesty, strength, and rule before all time, and now, and to the end of all time. Yes."* (Jude 24 MSG) How amazing is that; to know that God loves you, He alone has the power to present you pure, without fault, if we turn our life and our lifestyles over to Him.

But, in the meantime, if you have been sexually active and have not been tested for disease - get tested now. There are local health clinics that do confidential, free testing. You may find out that you have contracted a disease. That does not mean that God's grace will not cover you. It only means that there are consequences for the decisions that you made, and you have to live with those consequences. You have probably heard people quote the verse *"And we know that all things work together for good to them that love the Lord and are the called according to His purpose"* (Romans 8:28 KJV). You might think, "How can God use this mess for my good? I disobeyed him, so I don't understand that." It's so simple. We all have sinned and are not worthy to be in His presence. But just as God can save the person whose only sin was telling a lie, His grace also covers that young lady who has slept with every man on the planet. That's just another thing that is so great about our God!

If you don't get anything else, get this: the only way to protect yourself from the physical consequences of sex is to keep sex where God intended it to be - in the monogamous marital relationship between one male and one female, for life; and that's on period!

POP QUIZ TIME!!!

(I just gave you a whole lot of information.)*

1. Which group has the highest number of cases of chlamydia?
   A. Females ages 15 to 24.
   B. Males ages 15 to 24.
   C. Senior Citizens over 60
   D. Adults ages 30-50

2. As long as a person has no STI symptoms, they
   A. Cannot infect anyone else
   B. Don't have to worry, they aren't infected.
   C. Don't have to get tested
   D. None of the above

3. Which of these infections is curable?
   A. HIV
   B. Gonorrhea
   C. Genital Warts
   D. Herpes

4. You can get an STD even if you don't have vaginal sex.
   A. True
   B. False

5. How can you prevent yourself from getting an STI?
   A. Use a condom
   B. Don't mess with nasty boys
   C. Pray after you have sex
   D. Don't have sexual contact before marriage

*Answers: 1) A, 2) D, 3) B, 4) A, 5) D

31

Prayer for Me

Dear God,

It's me _____ .

I know that my body is your temple. You created me for your glory. Please keep me pure. Keep me set apart. I want to save my body for the husband that you are preparing for me. I do not want to have any "souvenirs" from past relationships. I don't want to have hard conversations with the man that will be my husband. Forgive me for what I may have done in the past. Purify not only my body, but also my mind and my soul. Don't let me believe the lies that the enemy is telling me. Thank you for hearing my prayer. Amen.

Dear Daughter,

This is a hard letter for me to write. I haven't seen you since you were a baby. I know that you might not understand but I want you to know that I loved you then and I love you now. Your mother and I didn't get along with each other because I was young and didn't want to be her boyfriend. I wanted to be in your life but since I didn't want her to be in a relationship, she stopped letting me see you. Her mother supported her with that. They moved away and didn't tell me where they were going. I was mad at first and I just said, "forget it." I tried to forget and go on with my life, but I couldn't. I tried to find you, but no one gave me any information. It was like you all just disappeared. Looking back, I should have tried harder, but I was young and didn't know how. I think about you every single day. I pray that the good Lord is looking out for you. Looking back, if I could tell you one thing, that's to pray and wait for God to send you a husband before you start having sex. That one decision changed my whole life. In life, there are no do-overs. If you haven't forgiven me, I hope that you will. I now have a beautiful wife and you have two brothers that I pray you will be able to meet one day.

Love always,
Dad

Chapter Four

"Slow Down. Adulthood Loading"

Run from anything that stimulates youthful lusts. Instead, pursue righteous living, faithfulness, love, and peace. Enjoy the companionship of those who call on the Lord with pure hearts
(2 Timothy 2:22)

"Why would I want to break up with him? Just because he's locked up is no reason to break up with him. We've been together for four years. He only got two years so when I graduate, he'll be out." "What is he locked up for?" "Selling drugs, but it was only weed; he shouldn't have been locked up." (Brittany, age 16)

"I've been with him so long; I don't know if I'll ever be able to find anybody else. I always run away from my problems so I'm not going to run just because he hits me sometimes. You don't know what it's like; I know what he's like and he might not be perfect, but I might find somebody who treats me worse than that." (Toni, age 16)

Adolescence! What a time! The highs, the lows, the mountaintop experiences, the valleys; it is the best of times and the worst of times! The teen years can be some of the most difficult years to go through. Everything is major: "What do I wear to the football game"; "I can't find a homecoming outfit"; "I can't believe you're wearing that – that went out of style two years ago." "Are you sure he was looking at me?" "Who is that girl in the picture with you on your Snap?" "I saw your Instagram," "I texted you, and you didn't text me back." Being a teen is somewhat like being a toddler going through the "terrible twos." On the one hand you are asserting your independence. You are making decisions about who to spend your time with, what to spend your money on, and what your plans are beyond high school and so many other things that you must decide. On the other hand, you still want to be the baby; you want an allowance; you want Mommy to cook and clean; you want Daddy to pay your cell phone bill, buy your clothes and to keep gas in the car. Well, it's the same way with your parents; sometimes they treat you like an adult (or expect you to act like an adult) and at other times, you are treated like a baby. What's a girl to do? On top of all this, your body has undergone changes and you really don't know what's going on. All of a sudden you are starting to look at boys in a different way; boys are starting to look at you in a different way. Could it be the ugly duckling has turned into that beautiful swan? This isn't like elementary school where relationships consisted of a handwritten note "I like you, do you like me" with the legendary two squares for the response: Yes or

No. If the answer was yes, then you were in a relationship. If it was no, then the note was passed on to the next boy. No, this isn't even like middle school where the relationship lasted for about a week; two weeks if it was a "serious" relationship. If you're lucky you might text occasionally, pass notes or send messages through your two best friends. In the serious relationships, you might even get a kiss on the stairs or after school. This is high school, the real thing. From the time you attended that first orientation, these words were echoed: "The 9th grade is the most important grade. What happens here is going to stay with you and ultimately will determine the course for the rest of your life!" If that's really true, then I've got to make good decisions. So now we have young people who have taken that the wrong way and have applied the idea to their intimate relationships. We have these couples walking around like they are in "mini- marriages" and cannot find a way out. I listen as students talk about upcoming birthdays and holidays and the gifts that they plan to give and receive cell phones, video game systems, diamond earrings, lingerie, North Face coats, Coach and Michael Kors bags and Ugg boots. Whatever happened to Teddy Bears, chocolates, and costume jewelry? Girls used to be taught that they could not accept certain gifts from a guy that they were not married to but that seems to have changed. Wouldn't you know that there are some parents doing just the opposite; they are encouraging their daughters to expect expensive gifts. I was pleasantly surprised when a young lady told me that her father would not allow her to keep a ring that she had been given as a gift. This leads me to the point of this chapter: The relationship that you have now is probably not the one that you will have ten years from now or even five years from now. You will continue to grow and change; he will grow and change. Yes, there are a few who will marry their high school sweethearts and live happily ever after, but not many. When the counselors were telling you that the 9th grade was a crucial year, they were mainly talking about academics. As we have seen, many young people have made decisions about their bodies that will stay with them for the rest of their lives, but the relationships that have been involved in these life-changing events are usually long over before the challenging part begins. I love this scene from a movie I saw once that went something like this: A teenage girl found out that she was pregnant and went to confront the boyfriend. He said that he wanted out of the relationship because he wanted to play football. She said to him, "I thought you said we'd be together forever." His reply was, "June to September, that's about forever to me." Most young men are not looking for long term relationships at this point. They may find themselves "going with" the same young lady for more than a year, but rarely is he faithful in the sense that females would like. Men think differently from women. Commitment in the mind of many teenage males does not mean

MEN THINK DIFFERENTLY FROM WOMEN!!!!

that he won't talk to other females, go out with other females or even become involved physically with another female; it just means that he has one "main" girlfriend, which back in the day it was called, "The main squeeze" (ask your parents about that).

Many teenagers get so deep into these relationships that they don't know how to end them. If you can remember that these relationships are not "til death do you part," you will be better off. If the relationship that you find yourself in is not making you a better person, then it should end. Like Brittany, at the beginning of this chapter, you might find yourself involved with someone who has little regard for the law and is, or has been, locked up. I'm going to suggest that now would be a good time to end the relationship. If you are serious about your life, then your values should be different from a person that has chosen a life of crime. If you are a Christian young lady, then the bible has already told you *"Don't become partners with those who reject God"* (2 Corinthians 6:14 MSG). In the case of young ladies who are in abusive relationships, be it physically, sexually or emotionally, please get out. It is not your job to rescue someone. It is so easy to get caught up in someone else's drama and make it your own. "You don't understand him; he doesn't have a father in his life; he only does this because he doesn't know what else to do; I'm all he's got." I might sound unsympathetic, but his problems are not your problems. You cannot solve his problems. You are only a child yourself. You can encourage him to get some help. You can introduce him to your pastor or someone else who might be able to help him; but that is not your job. He might try to make you feel guilty about ending the relationship if he has become emotionally dependent on you. But for your own sake, you need to let it go. We will explore abusive relationships later.

I can remember when I was younger, we were cautioned against becoming "too thick too quick." I see that happening all the time and that's why so many relationships are drama filled. Now maybe **you** are the one who is dependent on **him**. If you are a teenager, or even a single young adult, it is not the responsibility of your boyfriend to take care of you. That's the job given to your parents or your family.

Guys become possessive when they start giving you things. Our society has become so materialistic that many girls are only attracted to a guy based on what he can buy her. All too often, there is a big price tag attached. Take Stephanie, a sixteen-year-old high school student. She found herself on the wrong end of that type of relationship. Stephanie was asking Ramon to buy her clothes, shoes, food and to pay her phone bills. I tried to tell her that she was flirting with danger. She would tell me, "He wants to take care of me." I would ask, "What is he getting in return?" She would reply, "Nothing! He's just nice like that — he doesn't want anything, and I'm not giving him anything either. I wish he would try something with me." The more I talked, the more defensive she became. Then the time came where he was ready to cash in on his investment. She didn't want to go along with the plan, so she tried to break up with him. He wasn't going for that, so he started stalking her and harassing her. One day she came home and found him hiding in her basement. As scary as this was, thankfully it did not end in violence. This scene repeats itself daily all over America.

Young ladies, this is not what relationships are all about. I'm going to apologize to you for the fact that some of you have not seen a successful relationship close-up. Some women, many of which are single parents, will seek out men who can help them out financially without thinking about the negative example that is being set for the children in their home. Some daughters get the idea that this is what men are for. Some girls see their moms involved in bad, sometimes abusive relationships but stay in them because the man is giving them money.

A healthy relationship must be mutually satisfying for each of the partners in it. It has to be developed over time. I can recall when a student came to me one day pouring out her heart about this guy that I assumed she was dating. She told me that he was a co-worker, and their relationship was so magical. It was if they had always been meant to be together. They would talk for hours on end on the phone. They could finish each other's sentences. So, I'm thinking, "That's so nice." Her only concern was that he had a girlfriend, and she didn't know what to do. I asked her how long she and the boyfriend had been talking, and she said, "just since Saturday." This was Monday. I hated to be the bearer of bad news, but I had to gently tell her that she was not in a relationship. Healthy relationships begin slowly. Boy meets girl. Time should then be spent just getting to know that individual on a friendly basis. You may talk on the phone sometimes, hang out with friends (group dating), and go to school or other events. This time is necessary to determine whether or not this is a good person. You can learn some things about their values during this time. If things check out and you both feel that you're ready to become exclusive, then each person needs to agree to this and now you are in a committed relationship. This should take a few months. The problem with most teenagers, is that they skip the "getting to know you" stage and jump right into the physical part of the relationship, and this leads to disaster.

Whatever happened to the "first comes love, then comes

marriage, then comes junior in the baby carriage?" You may have never heard that little schoolyard rhyme, but the idea is still the one that goes along with God's plan for us. Think back to the "good touch – bad touch" lesson. When you start moving into the "bad touch" arena, problems can happen. Sexual emotions are the most powerful natural emotions that God has given us to experience. My Sunday School teacher, Uncle Ralph, used to tell us all the time, "The human body is a powerful thing." He always told us that we shouldn't even engage in premarital kissing because something that sensual can set the wheels in motion for something greater.

"God did not create us to touch personal parts of another person's body and then STOP -- any more than we were created to place chocolate in our mouth and not swallow!"

-Dr. James Dobson

I heard Dr. James Dobson say once, "God did not create us to touch personal parts of another person's body and then STOP -- any more than we were created to place chocolate in our mouth and not swallow!" The more sexually involved you become with someone, the more powerful those emotions become. I remember when I lived in Atlanta and would, at times, drive home to Cleveland. Coming around the Tennessee mountains you would see signs that said, "Runaway Lane" which was an extension of the highway that trucks could go

42

up if the driver found that he was losing control coming down the sometimes steep incline. You know where I'm going with this. That's how it is with physical involvement in relationships. The relationship which may have started slowly can often take off and almost spin out of control if there are no "runaway lanes" in place. I often wondered what would happen if the truck missed the runaway lane. God put "runaway lanes" in place for us. I Corinthians 10:13 reads: *"The temptations in your life are no different from what others experience. And God is faithful. He will not allow the temptation to be more than you can stand. When you are tempted, He will show you a way out so that you can endure"* which means that, yes, you may, or shall I say, you will, be tempted, but God ALWAYS will provide a way for you to get out of the situation. But you have to take some personal responsibility. Some girls like to "tease" men, which means they are flirting with them, often getting them aroused and perhaps making them believe that they are going to give them something that they aren't and unfortunately, some girls end up getting raped. Let me go on and say this now: your mouth does not belong on a guy's penis, period. If you know anything about the male reproductive system, think back to our runaway truck; once certain things are set in motion, they cannot be stopped. Before you twist my words, let me say right now that it is never okay for a man to force himself on a female, and no will **always** mean no, but females should be careful to not place a man in a compromising position. Several years ago, a professional athlete was charged with the crime of raping a young lady. He argued that it was consensual, but she cried rape. The important part of the story lies here: the athlete called the young lady, whom he had met earlier that day, who was staying at a neighboring hotel at 2:00 in the morning and asked her to come over to his hotel. Okay, I don't know if you got this. I'm going to repeat it: the athlete called the young lady at 2:00 in the morning and asked her to come over to his hotel. She came! What possibly was going through her head when she received that call? "Maybe he has some problems that I can talk to him about," "maybe he's lonely and just needs company," "Maybe …." See I can't even come up with any other possible, logical scenarios as to what she was thinking he wanted from her at 2:00 in the morning. Oh, I forgot the most logical one, "He knows that I'm a Christian and he wants me to share with him the plan of salvation." I don't think so. There is only one thing that a grown man has on his mind when he calls an 18-year-old female, who had been flirting with him earlier in the day, invites her to his hotel and room and she accepts the invitation, at 2:00 in the morning. He was convicted of the crime and served time in prison. Although she was the victim, I hope that she learned a valuable lesson from her actions, and you can too. I'm not going to be too hard on her because there, but for the grace of God, it could have been me.

I Corinthians 10:13 "...When you are tempted, he will show you a way out..."

When I was younger, I was attracted to professional athletes. I guess I was considered a groupie. I used to pride myself on being able to find creative ways to meet them, methods that would not make me look like a groupie so that my friends and I could get past the barriers and interact with them. The only difference between the other young lady and myself was that God was merciful. I was in situations where I could have been attacked, raped or forced to do things that I didn't want to do, but like I said, God spared me. The one time where I felt a little scared, he provided that runaway lane, and I took it. Yes, I was young and dumb, but I learned my lesson.

Remember, God's plan for you is to keep yourself pure, and that would include emotionally as well, for the person that he has reserved for you. What gift can you possibly expect to give the man that God has chosen for you if you have given so much of yourself to someone else?

Can you imagine what it would be like on Christmas morning when you went downstairs to open your gifts? You had made out a wish list, and you expected to receive what you asked for. You open the first box. Inside is one of your dirty shirts that has some stains on it and the collar is very dirty. You open the second package. Inside is a pair of your muddy shoes. You are starting to get mad. The next package is no better – a broken necklace. As the old people used to say, that's what happens when you put the cart before the horse. You've used up the gifts before Christmas so there is nothing new to get.

The Song of Solomon 4:1-7 paints a beautiful picture about the love between a man and a woman. The words just seem to flow off the page. Can you imagine yourself as the woman this man is talking about?

You are beautiful, my darling, beautiful beyond words. Your eyes are like doves behind your veil. Your hair falls in waves, like a flock of goats winding down the slopes of Gilead. 2. Your teeth are as white as sheep, recently shorn and freshly washed. Your smile is flawless, each tooth matched with its twin. 3. Your lips are like scarlet ribbon; your mouth is inviting. Your cheeks are like rosy pomegranates behind your veil. 4. Your neck is as beautiful as the tower of David, jeweled with the shields of a thousand heroes. 5. Your breasts are like two fawns, twin fawns of a gazelle grazing among the lilies. 6. Before the dawn breezes blow and the night shadows flee, I will hurry to the mountain of myrrh and to the hill of frankincense. 7. You are altogether beautiful, my darling, beautiful in every way.

How does that make you feel? This is someone who has taken the time to study you, to really get to know you, to develop a sincere love for you and anticipate the pleasure that you will bring him? Take the time and read the whole Song of Solomon.

One of the most precious modern-day love stories is between two of my favorite young people; John and Kimille. They made a vow to not even kiss before marriage. The morning of their wedding, he shared these words in a post.

"The day has come. My best friend in the world is coming home with me forever. We will worship and share our first kiss. We will enter holy covenant and celebrate with family and friends. We will finally taste the fruits of the marriage bed and spend the rest of our days as living examples of one timeless truth: With God ALL things are possible."

Can you imagine your future husband saying this about your marriage? In 2023, it is still possible!

Some teenagers have gotten so caught up in these relationships that the stress of the

break-ups have caused them to consider and attempt suicide. If you ever feel that way, please tell someone. The Bible says, *"weeping may last through the night, but joy comes with the morning"* (Psalm 30:5b) it also says, *"I will comfort them and exchange their sorrow for rejoicing"* (Jeremiah 31:13b). See, even God knows that we get discouraged and sometimes want to give up, so He gave us hope. If we know anything about the Lord, it is that He is always true to His word, and He loves you and cares for you very much.

I know what it's like to be a teenager. I also know what it's like to be an adult. Enjoy your youth! This is not the time to be stressing about all this relationship stuff. Remember that adulthood is coming. It's hard enough when you're grown, so take the time now to kick back, hang out and enjoy yourself. It's a time to really get to know who you are and who God wants you to be. This is a time to plan for your future. Don't cause yourself to miss out on opportunities because you have spent so much time and energy on the wrong things. Years from now you want to look back on these years and smile. The memories you want to tell your children and grandchildren about are being a cheerleader, starring in the school play, putting together a robot in the robotics club, volunteering at the local Food Bank. You want to develop friendships that might stay with you throughout life. Just remember, adulthood is loading and will be here soon enough!

Prayer for Me

Dear God,
It's me _____ .
Wow! There is so much in the Bible that I'm learning about relationships. I really want to live my life so that you are happy with me. I don't want to cheat myself out of having a godly relationship. I don't want to feel pressured into being in a relationship and doing things that I shouldn't do. Help me to not be jealous of other people in relationships. Help me to spend my time getting to know myself well and knowing you. It's sometimes hard because it seems like everybody has somebody, except me. I know that's exactly what the devil wants me to think, but I know better. Help me to surround myself with friends that share my values and also want to live to please you! I want to have a relationship like John and Kimille. I know that you can bless me like that when the time comes. I love you, and thank you for hearing my prayer.

Dear Baby Girl,

First, I want to tell you I am so PROUD of you!

You are the sunshine to my day, the joy in my heart and one of God's most beautiful blessings upon my life. The moment you were born, my life and heart changed forever. I am so thankful and honored to be your Daddy, friend, personal stand-up comedian, number one supporter and most of all your prayer partner and warrior. I pray for you all the time, and I ask God to keep you in His loving arms of protection every moment of your life.

You are my forever beautiful, smart, talented, unique, gifted, unparalleled, incomparable, matchless, and fearless daughter, no one can or will ever take those titles away from you because they are from my heart, and YOU ARE MY HEART!

There is no greater love than that of which a Daddy has for his daughter. I am so honored to be the self-proclaimed President & CEO of #GirlDad, Inc., and no one can take my place (smile). You are the epitome of a dream come true and the symbol of God's grace and mercy all wrapped into one.

You bring joy out of sorrow and peace from your soul with your illuminating SMILE (dimples included). You are my Baby Girl, and I love you beyond the moon and stars. Never forget the LEGACY within you, the BLESSINGS upon you and the amount of PRIDE I have by being blessed as your Father.

You are my daughter, and there can be no other!

Love, Daddy

Chapter Five
HELP, I MESSED UP!

I cried out, "I am slipping!" but your unfailing love, O LORD, supported me. When doubts filled my mind, your comfort gave me renewed hope and cheer. Psalm 94:18-19

Relax, it's really not the end of the world! Yes, you might find yourself in a very difficult situation. You've been watching the calendar. "I'm late." "My period should have been here by now." "Maybe it's because I have a cold." "Maybe the app is wrong, and it shouldn't even be time." You've had quite a few scenarios pass through your head, but the truth has finally won out. You think you're pregnant. "Oh Lord, what am I going to do? "My mama is going to kill me." Alright, slow down. Before you go any further, you need to know if you really are pregnant. Take a couple of dollars and go to the drugstore and buy a pregnancy test. Take it home and take it. If it's negative, you need to repeat the test in a couple of days, then if it's still negative you need to thank God, repent and promise that you won't get in this situation again. Now, if it's positive, there's no need to waste your money on more tests. These tests are pretty accurate. Unfortunately, there may be false negatives, but rarely is there a false positive. "So now what am I going to do?" I'm going to draw a little diagram and then talk about each of your options.

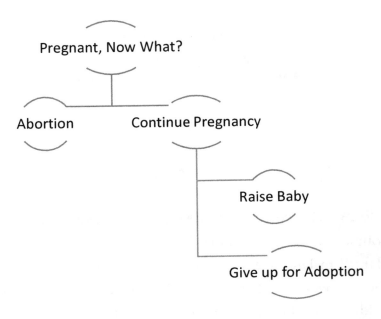

Before I go on, I don't want you to look at this chart and think that I am supporting abortion. Quite the opposite, I do NOT support abortion, but I want to put it here so that I can address the issue and let you see why abortion is not the easy option that the enemy would have you think.

This is a simple diagram, but it has tremendous consequences. Any decision that you make is not going to be easy, but once again, God promised that He would be with us and can take a seemingly bad situation and turn it around for your good and His glory.

"Mrs. Dixon, I need to tell you something. I'm pregnant. What am I supposed to do now? I can't have this baby. Do you know what my mother is going to say if she finds out? I should have never let him in the house. All I know is that I can't be pregnant. My mother doesn't even know I'm having sex."

I sat and listened as Tereia poured out her heart over her situation. She was pregnant and was struggling with what she was going to do. When she finally paused, I asked her why she was telling me. Yes, I was the "pregnancy" teacher, but she had already concluded that she was going to abort the life that was growing inside of her. She also knew how I felt about abortion. Luckily there was an agency across the street from the school that I could refer her to where they could counsel her more about the decision she wanted to make. Let's look closer at these options.

ABORTION

Perhaps you have considered abortion. I'll be honest, I believe that thought probably comes to the mind of every female that finds herself in an unplanned pregnancy situation. Some women are able to quickly dismiss the thought, but some manage to think about it long enough to be persuaded that it is actually a good option. This has been one of the most hotly debated issue in our society. I am always amazed at the conviction that students have when we talk about abortion and why it isn't an option for them. Most say that they believe that abortion is wrong, or that it is against their religion. I always come back and ask what their religion has to say about pre-marital sexual relations, and why can't they live with the same conviction? Hmm...? Alright, back to this abortion question. I'm convinced that so many people decide that it's an option because they don't really know what it's all about.

> We don't have to decide when life begins. God already made that decision!

"An abortion is the removal or expulsion of an embryo or fetus from the uterus, resulting in its death."

One of the big debates about abortion centers around the question, "When does life actually begin? The courts cannot even agree. While it is legal for a female to choose to end the life of her unborn baby; a person is charged with two counts of murder if they kill a pregnant female. Someone, somewhere must have decided that a baby growing inside of the womb is indeed a life. We don't need to decide when life begins, but accept what God has already shown, that life begins before birth. It is impossible to take a life before birth and be justified. God's ideals and ethics do not change based on the situation. Life always begins before birth in the eyes of God even if rape, incest, or other sinful acts conceived the baby.

Just so you can be informed, I want to explain some of the common abortion methods.

Dilation and Curettage (D & C)

The Cervix is dilated with a series of instruments to allow the insertion of a curette (a looped shaped steel knife). The unborn child is then cut into pieces and scraped from the uterine wall. There is usually a whole lot of blood. A nurse will normally reassemble the body parts to be sure that all are removed; otherwise, infection can set in.

Dilation and Evacuation (D & E)

This procedure is performed at 12 to 20 weeks. By week 12, the baby's bones are hardening and can no longer be pulled apart with suction. Abortion is now achieved by dismemberment. A seaweed-based substance, called *laminaria,* is inserted into the cervix, which causes dilation. The next day forceps with sharp metal teeth are inserted and parts of the baby's body are torn away with a twisting motion and removed piece by piece. At this age, the head is usually too large to be removed whole and must be crushed and drained before taken out. D & E's are preferred by abortion advocates because, unlike other second trimester methods, they insure the baby's death. The nurse then reassembles the body parts to be sure that all was removed.

Menstrual Extraction

A very early suction abortion, often done before the pregnancy test is positive.

"Morning After" Pill

Up to 72 hours after intercourse, a woman is administered large doses of birth control pills (or levonorgestrel, also known as Plan B) to prevent the embryo from implanting in the uterus wall. Twelve hours after the first dose, a second dose is given. Large doses of birth control pills work to prevent ovulation and hinder sperm motility.

Prostaglandin Chemical Abortion (RU-486)

This form of abortion uses chemicals which cause the uterus

to contract intensely, pushing out the developing baby. The contractions are more violent than normal, natural contractions, so the unborn baby is frequently killed by them -- some have even been decapitated. Many, however, have also been born alive.

Suction Curettage, or Vacuum Aspiration

The cervix is dilated as in a D & C, then a tube with a very sharp edge on the tip is inserted into the uterus and connected to a strong suction apparatus. The suction device, similar to a conventional vacuum cleaner but 29 times as powerful, tears the unborn child apart and sucks the pieces into a jar.

Because of the death and destruction of the fetus/baby, this is why, we as Christians, should not consider abortion as an acceptable option to pregnancy.

CONTINUE PREGNANCY

Now that we have ruled out abortion as an option, we are going to bring a baby into the world. I believe that this would be a good time for us to talk about the relationship that caused the pregnancy. There is a baby growing inside of you that has two parents. If you haven't already told the father, I'm thinking the time is now. The longer you wait, the harder it will be. Sadly, some of these conversations don't go so well. Usually, there is expressed doubt. *"It's not mine,"* or *"How do you know it's mine?"* If this is the reaction, he's probably speaking out of fear or disappointment and not actually doubting, unless he has a good reason to not believe you. If he truly feels that he is not the father, and you know for a fact that he is, then there's not much else you can do until the baby is born. There are some paternity tests that can be performed during pregnancy, but they can only be done with a doctor's consent and pose some risk to the baby. If he chooses not to participate in the pregnancy, then you must accept it. If he is a willing participant, then you two can proceed with the decision making. If you go back to the chart, you now are faced with two options: keep the baby and raise it yourself or give the baby up for adoption.

I want to talk about adoption. Where I live, on any given day, there are approximately 2,500 children in custody of the Family and Children's Services. This reflects a somewhat revolving door of children that can't be taken care of by their parents. The outcomes of these cases vary: some are eventually returned home; some remain in permanent custody of the county and at 18 "age out" of the foster care system; and some are adopted. Unfortunately, it takes the county at least 18 months to take away parental rights and assume custody of a child. In order for a child to be taken into custody in the first place, the child has to have been abused or neglected. This alone tells me that on any given day there are at least 2500 abused and neglected children in my county that need help. The newspaper is filled with stories daily where babies and children are being abused, sometimes fatally. One of the problems in the urban community is that mothers are not encouraged to give their

> Adoption GIVES life!
> Abortion TAKES life away!

babies up for adoption. I have had students say that they would rather have an abortion than to give their baby up for adoption. How selfish! Why would you choose death for a baby that God gave life to? They often say, "I'm carrying this baby for nine months; do you think I'm going to give it to a stranger?" My response is that "nine months is a far cry from 18+ years." My heart goes out for babies and children that I see in the stores and on the streets: dirty, uncared for, unloved, and trying to hustle to make their own way. I think about the home that they possibly could have had if their mother had not been so selfish in her thinking. There are so many "parents without children" that are waiting to give their love, time and resources to an innocent baby. My husband and I were in that situation. If a homeless, drug-addicted young lady living on the streets of Cleveland had decided to end her pregnancy, we would not be the proud parents today of a vibrant, beautiful, intelligent, talented, and outgoing young lady. As I watched her grow, I couldn't help but think where she would be if she had remained with her mother. Abortion takes away life; adoption gives life! There is no disgrace in saying that you are unable or unwilling to care for a child that you brought into this world. There is disgrace, however, in not caring for a child that you bring into this world. It takes so much to raise a child these days. It's hard enough for two parents to raise a child, so there is no question the struggle can be greater for a single, young mom." There are two main types of adoption that are available today:

- A **closed adoption** is one where generally no identifying information about the birth family or the adoptive family is shared between the two, and there is no contact between the families. The adoptive family receives general information about the child and birth family before the child joins the family. After the adoption is finalized, the records are sealed. Depending on local law and what paperwork was signed and filed when the adoption was finalized, these records may or may not be available to the adopted child when they reach 18.

- An **open adoption** allows for some form of association among the birth parents, adoptive parents and the child they adopted. This can range from picture and letter sharing to phone calls, to contact through an intermediary or open contact among the parties themselves.

These are both good options and with the help of your parents, or other trusted adults, you and the baby's father need to decide what you think is best for your situation. If you do choose this option, make sure that you have the consent of the father, even if you aren't talking to him. Legally, he has to sign away his rights. There are obviously pros and cons to both arrangements. I have seen it work both ways with great results. The main thing is that you need to be comfortable with your decision. Although you shouldn't let someone "guilt" you into making a decision, if you are a minor, your parent's opinion will weigh heavily during this process.

By now you have weighed your options and have decided to join the ministry of motherhood. What do I mean by that? Motherhood is ordained by God and part of His plan. Therefore, God

> God holds motherhood in high regard!

59

holds motherhood in high regard, and we should too. Becoming a mother is not something to be taken lightly or for granted. Motherhood is a gift, but a gift that brings with it a tremendous responsibility. Although the world does not hold mothers in high regard, God does. With that being said, what can you do to prepare yourself for this awesome career?

1) **Learn!**

   There are so many resources available that can prepare you for pregnancy and the day-to-day tasks of motherhood. Maybe your school has a parenting class. Talk to your mother, aunts or other mothers you know that can share their wisdom with you. The library is full of books, and there are so many wonderful websites that can provide you with a wealth of knowledge about pregnancy and parenting.

2) **Make a financial plan.**

   Make no mistake about it, babies cost money. It is never too soon to begin thinking about childcare options (your biggest expense) and health care.

3) **Take care of your body**.

   Make sure that you keep your regular doctor's appointments and listen to what they have to say. Among other things, eat a balanced diet and get proper rest. If you use alcohol, tobacco or other drugs, please stop.

4) **Ask God for His forgiveness.**

   I've seen too many girls turn their back on God during this time. Maybe it's because of the way church people look at them with disappointment. Unfortunately, people can say and do some unkind things. But remember, everyone makes mistakes. We don't always see everyone's mistakes, but God knows. If you're going to be a mother, you need to commit your life and your baby to the Lord. It is difficult to take this journey only on your own strength. Use your situation as an opportunity to share with other girls the risks of not doing things God's way. There used to be a time when pregnant girls were forced to go down to the altar and ask God and the church for forgiveness. I believe that the Lord will lead you to do what needs to be done. You must also be ready to accept discipline. You might not be able to be on the worship team, sing in the choir, or hold leadership positions for a period of time. This is no reason to leave the church. Use this as a time for self-reflection, planning and growth.

5) Be prepared for negativity.
We live in a "double-minded" world. Our nation worships the sex god. Sex is used to sell everything. We can't turn on TV without sex, in all of its perversions, but pregnant teens are still looked down upon. When my students do the Baby-Think-It-Over parenting simulation project with the electronic dolls, part of the assignment is to talk about the reactions from others when they are out in public. Many of the girls talk about how people gave them disapproving looks. Some have been asked their age but without follow-up questions. By contrast, when the boys have the babies, people compliment them and say encouraging words to them; some have even gotten baby-sitting offers. That's just the way it is!

Nicole grew up in foster care. When she turned 16, the county no longer sought a permanent home for her, but put her in transitional housing, which was supposed to prepare her for life on her own. When she turned 17, they gave her an apartment. A social worker would meet with her periodically, but basically, she was on her own. She soon became pregnant and had a son. She, herself, liked to drink and smoke, and her apartment became the spot where her friends came to smoke and drink. By this time, she had graduated and although I didn't see her often, I would still hear about her apartment. One day she came to the school, and I confronted her about what I had been hearing. She laughed it off and said, "they don't smoke around the baby; I keep him in another room." I reached out to her social worker to tell her my concerns. I'm not sure what became of them. Two years later I ran into Nicole again at the hospital. She said that she had just given birth to another son and invited me up to see the baby. When I got up to the room, the nurse was holding the baby, and he was wrapped in a blanket. Nicole then said, "He only has one hand." I didn't believe her because she was slightly laughing when she said it. I looked at the nurse, and the nurse nodded yes. Then Nicole said, "He's also missing some toes." The nurse nodded again. "He was also born with a cleft palate (a birth defect that occurs when the mouth does not form properly during pregnancy)." I was speechless and mad, all at the same time. All of this could have been avoided. I took Nicole out into the hallway and let her know how disappointed I was. She said that she had stopped smoking when she found out that she was pregnant, and maybe she did. What some don't realize is the baby is completely formed by the end of the first 12 weeks of pregnancy, often before the mother even knows she is pregnant, and any damage that's been done cannot be reversed. I told her that I would be praying for her and especially for the baby. I'm still praying.

"Help! I messed up!" That right there is a prayer that you can pray. God would never turn His back on you. Talk to him, lean on him. You will get through this!

Prayer for Me

Dear God,

It's me _____.

Help! I messed up! I got caught up and now I'm pregnant. It's one thing to disappoint myself and my parents, but I disappointed you too. But, I'm glad that you still love me and are here to help me. First I want to ask you to forgive me. Some people only ask for forgiveness when they get pregnant, but I'm asking you to forgive me for having sex without being married. I want you to help me to make the best decision for this baby that is growing inside of me. I know that this baby is created in your image. You know all about his/her future and I want to do everything that I can to make sure that he/she grows to know you and to love you. Lord, there are so many things that I have to think about and deal with, but I know with you I am not alone. Help me to be a good mother.

Dear Daughters-

Your mother and I were so excited when we started this journey with children. I cannot forget the moment I first heard your heartbeats. I think my heart leapt as fast as yours. But then I was nervous when I discovered you would be girls. The only thing that I knew about girls is what boys think about them. I immediately decided that my first job would be your protector. I remember the moments that you arrived just like it was yesterday. Even a little peep would make me jump to your attention. I wanted to be sure that you had everything that you needed and even more.

So, my second job was your provider. I have loved every moment together from the tea parties in our living room to the soccer games and dance recitals. Another one of my jobs then is your cheerleader. I hope that you have always known that you have me in your corner. Some of my favorite times though are the conversations we have in the car or around the dinner table.

One of my other jobs is to be your confidante. I hope that you know that I am always here to listen no matter the topic, no matter the time. You have no idea how proud I am of the young women that you have become. You are smart and confident in a way that I could not have imagined when you were tiny babies that I could hold in the palm of my hand. In that way, you have been my teacher. I have learned so much from you. You have made me want to be a better person, to be a better role model so that you know what is to be expected from your life partners. I could never have imagined how much better my life is with you, and I can only imagine what your future holds.

I hope that I have given you the tools to create the best life that you can have moving forward. In that way, my job has been to put you on the best possible path. I have enjoyed being your guide thus far, and I cannot wait to see where your paths will take you.

Love,
Daddy

Chapter Six

STICKS AND STONES
WILL BREAK MY BONES
(BUT EVEN THE WORDS CAN HURT)

… He will give a crown of beauty for ashes, a joyous blessing instead of mourning, festive praise instead of despair…. Isaiah 61:3

"Looking back on the whole situation, I should have seen it coming. People tried to tell me, but I wouldn't listen. Everything was perfect at the beginning. His mother was a friend of my father, and they introduced us. We were together ever since we were twelve. I waited three years before I had sex with him. I loved him, and he loved me. Everybody was jealous of our relationship because we were both cute, and he was always with me. His mother loved me just like a daughter. My family loved him too. We had it all worked out. We were going to graduate from high school and get married. I was sixteen when I got pregnant. Some of the people at church were surprised because I was so active in the church. I love to sing. I sang in the choir, and they always wanted me to sing solos. They thought I was a "good" girl. I was. I just had one boyfriend, and we were eventually going to get married. In school, he walked me to all my classes. Especially when I got big, he was there so no one would bump into me in the hallway. My relationship wasn't like everybody else's. I think the girls in my class were jealous of me because all their boyfriends were acting up. Every day they would complain about what their boyfriends were not doing. Many of their relationships ended while they were pregnant. Not mine.*

His aunt gave me a baby shower, and I got so much stuff. When the baby came, it was so perfect. Brad was over every day. He brought gifts for the baby, and he brought gifts for me. He would come over every day after school and feed the baby and sit with us. It was the perfect relationship. After the summer, school started back, and I returned to classes. It all started because I wasn't pregnant anymore, so I went back to wearing my regular clothes. I got really big when I was pregnant, but I lost all the weight, and I was back down to about 115 lbs. I didn't wear clothes that were revealing, but guys found me attractive. I was in love, and I didn't pay any attention to the guys that would try to talk to me. Brad was jealous. He started telling me that he only wanted me to wear big t-shirts and baggy warm-up pants. I did it. We would go places, guys would look at me and he would yell at me like I had done something to make them look at me. Girls would look at him, too, but I didn't care. He was cute, but I knew that he was mine. Soon I got tired of it and wanted to break up with him.

We sat down with the teacher to see if we could work things out. We had a good conversation and decided that we would try to make the relationship work because we really did love each other. That didn't work though. He kept accusing me of being unfaithful when I wasn't. I heard that he was seeing other girls, too. Finally, we just decided to leave it alone. That's where the trouble started. I couldn't stand to be away from him, and he couldn't stand to be away from me. I saw him with other girls, and I got jealous. I would follow him around the school.

One day I got mad, and I hit him in the head with a shoe. I got suspended from school. When I got back from my suspension, I was still mad at him, so I tracked him down and hit him again. He would call me on the phone and curse at me. He would drive by my house with his friends to see if I was home. He stopped buying things for the baby. I didn't get child support because I was in love with him, and I got mad with anybody who suggested that I should file to get child support. I thought that if I filed for child support, I would be hurting him. I wasn't thinking about the baby.

The incidences of violence continued. I would hit him, and he would hit me back. We both got arrested for domestic violence. Before it was time for him to go to court, he pretended to want to get back with me. I believed him and thought that we had mended our relationship. I started having sex with him again. When we got to court, he told the judge that we had fixed our relationship and everything else was a big misunderstanding. The judge asked me, and I told him that was true. When we left the court, he and his friends were laughing at me because he had played me. I was mad, no, I was furious. I still was in love with him, but I wanted to hurt him like he had hurt me.

The fights continued. I was almost kicked out of school because I kept getting suspended for fighting him or cutting class so I could follow him around. The charges against me were dropped. I finally have gotten over him. I found somebody new, so I don't think about him anymore. He still doesn't do anything for the baby, so I guess I will go and file for child support. I look back and think about the people who tried to talk to me, but I wouldn't listen. I thought I knew it all. I guess I didn't." - Kayla, age 17

"It's not worth it. If I could turn the clock back about three years, things would be different. I know you and everybody else tried to tell me, but y'all just didn't understand. Being locked up allowed me to think about what happened in my life. I have a little sister, and I hope she learned from my mistakes. I don't know if I'll get my daughter back. I have messed up every relationship that should be important to me. I turned on my mother and father. I messed up in school by missing so much. I have bruises and marks from black eyes, beatings and stab wounds that I got from my boyfriend. Don't think that he

doesn't have marks on him, too. I said that when I got out of here it's going to be different. I'm going to finish school and get my life together. "

- Faith, age 18 (after being released from a Youth Correctional Facility)

One day in my Teen Parent class, a student was preparing for a debate in her English class. The topic was "Is it Okay for a Man to Hit a Woman?" I didn't see where this would be much of a debate, but I allowed her time to get input from her classmates. The dialogue went something like this:

Girl: "Sometimes girls make them mad, and they have to hit her."

Girl 2: "Yeah, and sometimes girls be hitting on them, and they have to hit them back.

Teacher: "Well, I don't think that it's right for a female to hit a male any more than it is acceptable for a male to hit a female"

Girl 1: "Well, if he hits her back, that will teach her to not hit him."

Girl 3:" She shouldn't be doing things that make him mad."

Teacher: "So, it's okay if she makes him mad?"

All Girls: "Yes."

Needless to say, I was shocked by this dialogue. I couldn't think of any circumstances in which young ladies would think that physical abuse was acceptable or even justified. Ladies, there is no such thing as acceptable or justifiable abuse.

Unfortunately, I could spend this whole chapter storytelling. There is a trend that is sweeping America. More teens are involved in abusive relationships than ever before. Girls as young as 12 and 13 are in unhealthy relationships. I'd like to share a bit more about Faith. Faith was in an abusive relationship, but she felt that since they "fought each other," it was okay. She constantly would tell me that I didn't understand the love that she had for Jimmy. She said that the sex was so good that it was worth the fights and the pain that she had to put up with being in the relationship. There was nothing anyone could say to her that would make her change her mind. She spent many days in and out of the Juvenile Detention Center for fights that she had with her parents over the relationship. There were restraining orders to keep Faith and Jimmy apart, but she would disregard them and sneak out the house just to be with him. Custody of their child was eventually taken away due to her destructive lifestyle. She finally was sent away for a year when the situation deteriorated beyond repair. Thankfully the time that she had away gave her a chance to reflect on her life and her plans for the future. Faith's home life was not a factor in the decisions she made. She had two very well-respected, professional parents who cared a great deal for her. I talked to them a lot. They both said they cared for their daughter a great deal. Faith did not grow up in an abusive home or in a home where alcohol and drug use was present. The decisions that she made were decisions that she made based on the people that she associated with.

Abuse is a pattern of physically and emotionally violent and coercive behavior that one person uses to exercise power over another. Abusive relationships are unhealthy relationships. Abuse can fall under several categories:

Verbal

- Name calling
- Yelling
- Threatening to hurt or kill
- Criticizing appearance
- Belittling accomplishments
- Constant blaming

Emotional Abuse

- Apologizing and making false promises to end the abuse
- Ridiculing, blaming
- Accusing of cheating
- Monitoring conversations
- Embarrassing in front of others
- Constant phone calls and texts
- Posting embarrassing things about you on social media
- Making you account for your time
- Stalking
- Any controlling or manipulative behaviors

Physical Abuse

- Restraining or holding you down
- Hair pulling
- Poking or grabbing
- Biting
- Hitting
- Slapping
- Choking or strangling
- Throwing or hitting with objects
- Using a knife or gun

Resource Abuse

- Making you account for your expenditures (needing to know how you spend your money)
- Destroying property
- Taking keys/purse
- Sabotaging work or school

Sexual Abuse

- Constant sexual demands
- Forcing unwanted sexual acts
- Calling fat or ugly
- Forcing pregnancy or abortion

Many of you reading this have looked at your own relationships and have seen some of these behaviors present. You might even be thinking that just because he hit you only once, or he yells at you only when you make him mad that you're not in an unhealthy relationship. Some of you think that it's cute that he bought you a cell phone, and he texts you and calls you constantly.

When you are in a healthy relationship you do NOT have to walk on eggshells around your partner.

You might think he is just a caring guy when he tells you what and what not to wear. All these behaviors are signs of unhealthy relationships. Healthy relationships are based on mutual respect and trust. A healthy relationship lifts you up and doesn't tear you down. It makes you feel good about yourself and the people around you. When you are in a healthy relationship, you do not have to walk on eggshells around your partner. Everyone deserves to be in a healthy and positive relationship that is free from peer pressure and manipulation. Abusive relationships are based on manipulation, pressure and force, and they are unhealthy! If you can learn these lessons in your youth, it will save you much heartache in the future.

I'd like to share with you from my own personal experience. I was in an abusive relationship. Most people wouldn't think of it as such because I was not physically or sexually abused, but this individual was emotionally abusive towards me, which is just as bad, if not worse. I found myself involved with an individual who grew up in a very dysfunctional family. He had a heart of gold, but he did not know how to care for me in an appropriate way. He never saw a healthy relationship modeled while he was growing up. He was very paranoid and questioned the people I spoke to, hung around and even worked with. He was very jealous without cause. He would get mad over little insignificant things, yell and then give me the silent treatment. Each time we went out on a date it usually ended with him not talking to me because he would get mad at me for something. It eventually progressed to the point where I got sick when I'd think about him coming over to see me. I ignored many of the signs

early in the relationship thinking that he just needed a lot of understanding, and I could help him overcome some of his shortcomings. During the process, I became an unhappy person. I put on a front for my family and friends because I was ashamed of myself for continuing in a relationship that I knew was unhealthy and unsatisfying. At one point we broke up, for good reason. We eventually got back together because he started sending flowers and calling and apologizing (a trait of an abuser). After prayer and fasting, I was able to end the relationship for good. The sad part of the story is that he called himself a Christian. Just because a person claims that they are a Christian, doesn't necessarily mean that they are. I was an adult and should have gotten out of the relationship long before I did. It is not always easy to get out of a bad situation, but for your own sake, you have too. You deserve the best, so take care of yourself. Abuse in any form is unacceptable. Some of the warning signs that exist that are common in abusive relationships are as follows:

- **Dating an older Guy** – Many girls say that guys their own age are immature and that older guys know how to treat them better. The fact is that an older guy has more power than you do. They are more likely to have more sexual experiences and are more likely to pressure you to have sex and get you pregnant or to give you a sexually transmitted disease. Just because a guy is older doesn't make him more responsible, and it doesn't mean that you will be treated better.

- **Alcohol, Drugs and Sex** – These are a deadly combination. Using alcohol and drugs makes it harder for you to think clearly, it reduces your ability to assess a dangerous situation clearly and can reduce your ability to defend yourself from sexual assault.

● **A Past of Battering** – If he or she hit before, they will hit again. Many try to tell the new partner that they hit the previous person because they were provoked, or the other person deserved it. They will then go on to say that you're not like that person, and they would never, ever hit you. Remember this, if they hit before, they will hit again!

● **Jealousy** – Initially, you may think that this is cute and flattering. He is overly attentive and concerned with you. He wants to be with you all the time. He will say that this jealousy is a sign of love; don't be fooled. This is a sign of insecurity and possessiveness. He will question your whereabouts, accuse you of flirting, be jealous of the time you spend with friends, family and even children. This can escalate into the stalking or other controlling behaviors and can lead to other forms of abuse.

● **Family Background** – Most batterers were raised in abusive homes. Being raised in an abusive home undermines basic feelings of security, safety, trust, love and belonging. As a child, he may have never learned to deal with anger appropriately. Get to know the person that you are involved with. I don't want anyone to misunderstand; just because a person grew up in an abusive home won't necessarily make them an abusive person; it has just been shown that most abusers have come from abusive homes. The more information you have, the better.

- **A Tale of Two Cities:** "It was the best of times; it was the worst of times." Many females are confused by the sudden mood swings - one minute he's sweet, and the next minute he explodes. These relationships follow the pattern of "storm, then honeymoon." He never meant to hurt you. He may blame it on something that happened during the day. Many women stay in abusive situations because they enjoy the "honeymoon" period that follows the abuse. He may buy her expensive gifts, send flowers, take her on exotic vacations or just do all the things that she likes. In adolescent relationships, it is no different. Guys apologize profusely, promising that they will NEVER again repeat the abusive behavior. This is a very hard relationship to try to break out of because of the unpredictability of his personality.

So just how bad is this problem?

- One in three teenagers report knowing a friend or peer who has been hit, punched, kicked, slapped, choked or physically hurt by their partner.
- One in four teenage girls who have been in relationships reveal they have been pressured to perform oral sex or engage in intercourse.
- More than one in four teenage girls in a relationship (26%) report repeated verbal abuse.
- If trapped in an abusive relationship, 73% of teens said they would turn to a friend for help, but only 33% who have been in or known about an abusive relationship said they have told anyone about it.

- Nearly 80% of girls who have been physically abused in their intimate relationships continue to date their abuser.
- Of the girls between the ages 15-19 murdered each year, 30% are killed by their husband or boyfriend.
- Teens report dating abuse via technology is a serious problem. This includes spreading rumors about them on cellphones and social media apps and sharing private or embarrassing pictures/videos.
  - Cell phone calls and texting at unimaginable frequency means constant control day and night.

1 in 4

teens in a relationship communicated with their partner via phone or texting HOURLY between midnight and 5 AM

1 in 3

teens say they are messaged 10-30 times per hour asking where they are, what they're doing and who they're with.

Wow, this is a huge problem. If you find yourself in this situation, get help. You have your whole life ahead of you! In extreme cases, the abuser is so confused in the head that violence may erupt if you try to end the relationship. Now is not the time to keep secrets from your parents. If you find yourself scared and not sure how the relationship will end, don't hesitate to ask for help. You can talk to your parents, teachers, counselors or other trusted adults. Whatever you do, do not try to go it alone if you are fearful. I know that the movies encourage women to take matters into their own hands, but that's not reality. A bit closer to reality is the Lifetime movies that deal with the subject which often don't have the happy endings, because they are often based on real stories.

Adults and other adolescents are often unaware that teens experience dating violence. In a nationwide survey, 9.4 percent of high school students report being hit, slapped, or physically hurt on purpose by their boyfriend or girlfriend in the 12 months prior to the survey. About one in five women and nearly one in seven men who ever experienced rape, physical violence, and/or stalking by an intimate partner, first experienced some form of partner violence between 11 and 17 years of age.

- Both male and female adolescents report being victims of physical violence in relationships.

- Many relationships involve mutual abuse, with both partners using physical violence against the other, but females suffer more and are more likely to have serious injuries.

- Males, on the other hand, often say that the attacks didn't hurt and that they found the violence amusing.

- Adolescent girls who reported abuse from dating partners have been found to be at a much higher risk for a broad range of serious health concerns. These risks included being more likely to: (1) use alcohol, tobacco, and cocaine, (2) unhealthy weight control practices, (3) engage in sexual health risk behavior, including first intercourse before the age of 15 years with multiple partners, (4) have been pregnant, and (5) seriously consider or attempt suicide.

● Many of the risks associated with experiences of either physical or sexual dating violence were heightened for adolescent girls who reported both forms of abuse.

Now it isn't exactly clear whether dating violence places these girls more at risk or whether these problem behaviors make these girls more vulnerable to domestic violence or if there are other factors involved. What is clear is adolescent girls that have experienced dating violence engage in several problem behaviors that put them at risk for negative outcomes ranging from contracting HIV to pregnancy and suicide.

I need you to remember that you were created in the image of God, for His glory and He desires to see you whole. I don't think that I have to tell you that you are precious to Him and to me. So then, just how can you get out of this mess? First of all, pray about it. Trust me, God wants to help you. You have to realize that leaving the relationship will be hard, but trust in yourself and those around you. Constantly remind yourself of the reasons why you wanted to leave in the first place and why this relationship was harmful, not helpful. During this time your emotions may be out of whack and you may feel sad, lonely and even angry, however, remind yourself that these feelings are normal and that it is okay to be upset. You may even feel like you made a mistake. **It is never a mistake to get out of an unhealthy dating relationship.** Talk to friends, family or seek professional help to assist you in making sense of your feelings. Doing this will help you understand that the abuse was not your fault. Try keeping yourself busy with things that are important to you such as school, sports and extra-curricular activities. You will soon find out how busy and healthy your life can be once you have left the relationship! Make this time about yourself and treat yourself well. Go to the spa, have a girl's night out, hang out with friends, learn a new hobby or spend time with your family. If you have a little sister, she will love the attention. You deserve to feel good! If you know someone that is in an abusive relationship, be a friend and try to encourage them to get out. Now is not the time to keep secrets. You can help save their life. If they won't listen, tell your parents, teacher or another trusted adult. Remember: it is always better to be safe than sorry.

If you ask God to take control of your relationships, the story can have a happy ending. He can make your situation right. Isaiah 40:29-31 tells us *"He gives power to the weak and strength to the powerless. Even youths will become weak and tired, and young men will fall in exhaustion. But those who trust in the Lord will find new strength. They will soar high on wings like eagles. They will run and not grow weary. They will walk and not faint."*

Along with what we have discussed about unhealthy relationships there is another big potential problem area, the internet! The internet is great! You can do so much without ever leaving your home. However, for all the good that's on there, there is so much that's not good. You must use good sense to keep yourself safe while surfing. We seem to forget that the "don't talk to strangers" rule still applies:

- **NEVER** share your personal identifying information: your name, address, phone number – I know this gets tricky with apps like Instagram, Twitter, Snapchat and Facebook – but somehow young people don't recognize their vulnerability when they start posting photos and other information on the web.

- **NEVER** send pictures or videos of yourself with no clothes on to anyone!

- **NEVER** agree to meet someone that you meet online unless you have mutual friends who can vouch for the person's credibility and then meet them in a public place or with your mutual friend.

- **NEVER** tell strangers where you hang out, who your friends are, etc.

- **NEVER** assume that the person on the other end of your communication is who they say they are. There are MANY, MANY individuals that misrepresent themselves looking to meet teen girls. Don't automatically believe what someone's profile says. ANYBODY can create a profile and put whatever information on there they want.

If in doubt, or in danger, please tell your parents or someone in authority. This could literally be a life-or-death situation.

WHEN THINGS GO TERRIBLY WRONG

Occasionally in relationships, things can go terribly wrong. One day I was stunned by the following news headline, **"Cleveland Heights woman found dead in garbage can was shot, stabbed."** As horrible as this was, my reaction quickly went from stunned to baffled to anger. The victim was one of my girls. I immediately pictured her in the seat that she would always sit in;

the stories that she would tell, and the zest for life that she had. I remembered her first pregnancy. I remembered how she shared that she lost weight over the summer simply by stopping drinking soda and other sugary drinks. I remembered discussions about her family. I remembered laughing when she told stories about her friends. I remembered… and as much as I didn't want to replace those memories, new images emerged. Her name was Miriam; I say her real name because I don't want her to be forgotten. Miriam's young life was cut short by a man that said that he loved her. He fathered three of her four children. Their relationship had been marked by unthinkable violence. He had been arrested several times during their relationship for domestic violence. The account of the most recent charge, prior to her murder, she stated that she had been knocked unconscious and when she came to, she was soaking wet. He told Miriam that he had urinated on her. I am just sharing the facts here because I can't offer explanations or suggestions as to how a relationship deteriorates to this level. I can only wonder why the relationship didn't end after the first child or even the second child. As if the heinous abuse was not enough, her life had come to an end like this: stabbed in the torso, arms and legs; shot in the back of her head; stuffed into a garbage can; doused in bleach and discarded in the yard of an unoccupied house.

Again, I'm left speechless. Violence should not occur in a relationship. I pray that I never, ever have to hear a story like that again. This was never, ever, God's design for relationships. I beg you to never continue in a relationship that even has hints of violence. There are always red flags; please don't ignore them. If you are a Christian, pray and ask God to send you a mate; a man of His choosing. You are precious to Him and He only wants the best for you. Proverbs 3:5-6 says, *"Trust in the Lord with all your heart, and lean not to your own understanding. In all your ways acknowledge Him and He will direct your paths."* In other words, when you wait and trust God to send you the right person, to guide you in your relationships, He will lead you to the right situation. When we trust only in our own judgement and wishes, and take God out of the equation, it often leads to destruction.

Prayer for Me

Dear God,
This is a lot for me to take in. I had no idea that so many people are in abusive relationships, especially people my age. Please keep me from these kinds of relationships. I want to wait for the person that you will be happy with. Help me to pay attention to any red flags and get out of unhealthy relationships. Surround me with people that I can talk to if I ever feel afraid. I also want to be able to help my friends if they are ever in this situation. Thank you for loving me!

Chapter Six: Sticks and Stones Will Break My Bones

Dear Daughters,

I just turned 50! I know I don't seem that old, but I am 50! My life was forever changed when both of you were born. I never imagined that God would bless me with two amazing daughters. I am proud to be your father and I always brag about the two of you. As both of you enter your college years here is my Top Ten List on how to have an amazing life.

1. You do not need a man to complete you. When God made you, he made you complete. A man cannot make you happy. A man can enhance your happiness. You must find happiness within yourself, that way you aren't always looking thirsty.

2. Dress modestly. I know it may be fashionable to wear clothes that expose body parts but understand you don't have to do that to get attention. If you use your body to get men, then you must use your body to keep them. You want to be attractive without being an attraction.

3. Sex should be the dessert not the appetizer. Sex does not make a relationship better. In fact, it makes it worse. Don't believe the hype. Most men aren't looking for sex, but they will take it if offered.

4. When you go out on a date or to hang out with a guy take your own money. You don't need a man to buy you dinner or wherever y'all go. Men have a tendency to get possessive over stuff like this. When you have your own money it sends a strong message.

5. If you are dating someone, ask your friends and family what they think of him. Their opinion matters because they know you. If you are dating someone and you feel the need

85

to hide him because you know your friends and relatives won't like him, then he may not be the person for you.

6. If you are on a date and you feel uncomfortable go to the bathroom and call a friend or call an Uber. Trust your instincts and get out of there. You don't owe him an explanation.

7. You will experience a hard break-up at some point in your life. It will hurt. You will cry. And you will think that you can't get over it. But you will. It may take some time, but you will. Remember this, as long as you aren't married to him, or you don't have kids with him you can move on. If someone wants to break up with you—just thank them. If you try to convince someone to stay with you then you are opening up yourself to abuse.

8. Relationship mistakes are inevitable. You will make mistakes, but you will recover from them.

9. Be patient. God has somebody for you. I believe that. Don't get frustrated, desperate, or thirsty. Men often take advantage of needy women.

10. Dream big and go for your wildest dreams. Your dreams should be destined to fail unless God intervenes. If you make God proud, he will bless you.

Love,
Dad

Chapter Seven
OVER THE RAINBOW

"But 'God made them male and female' from the beginning of creation. 'This explains why a man leaves his father and mother and is joined to his wife, and the two are united into one."
Mark 10:6-8

"My mother said I could be anything I wanted when I grew up, so I wanted to be a lesbian" Tammy, age 19

It was the first day of the new semester. The time had come for my parenting class. In walked Tatiana. I took one look at her and said to myself, "Why is she in here – she will never be a parent." She had her hair cornrowed to the back; she had on a pair of long baggy jean shorts, a white tee and a pair of sneakers. She proceeded to slouch in the chair and put her legs up on the desk. As I took the attendance the other students responded when I read their names. I got to her name and read, "Tatiana Willis." There was no response. Other students said, "She's here, that's her (pointing)" I again said, "Tatiana Willis." She then responded with, "That's not my name. My name is Tee." So, I said, "alright Tee" and I asked her to put her feet on the floor. She rolled her eyes and put her feet on the floor. I knew that this was going to be a long semester. I thought about asking her counselor to remove her from the class, but I didn't. She behaved as I thought she would: doing very little work, being disruptive and inattentive, while her groupies would wait outside the door for her to come out.

Elena came to the teen parent class pregnant, like most of the other girls. Daily they would talk (or rather complain or vent) about their "baby daddy's": what they were doing, what they weren't doing, etc. Elena usually remained quiet. One day I realized why. It was Elena's birthday, and by that time she was very pregnant. She came to school wearing a t-shirt that had an air-brushed design of a heart and inside the heart it said, "Elena and Jay 4-ever." Elena was indeed pregnant by a young man, but she was a lesbian, or bi-sexual and her "girlfriend" Jay was another girl in the school; talk about confusion. Did I mention that her father was a minister?

Shelby had a very promising future. In high school she was a model student. She had the lead in the school play. She was in the choir; she played the flute in the orchestra. She was active in student government, worked on the yearbook staff and got excellent grades. She kept herself very fit, dressed nicely and always had her hair done. It was no surprise that she went away to college on a full scholarship. She completed the first year and returned for the second year. She soon came home after finding that she was pregnant. She had a beautiful bouncing baby girl. She and the dad were living together. After a while, he moved out. Things started to turn then. Shelby began a total transformation; she stopped going to school, the times I saw her, her hair was rarely combed, she didn't seem to care about her body and she was now proclaiming that she was liberated and was going to be a lesbian.

God put a rainbow in the sky as a sign of a covenant with Noah that He would never again destroy the whole world with water. It was a sign of peace. When my daughter was younger, she would light up when she was outside after a down pouring of rain, and she could see a rainbow in the sky. We were at the store one day, and we were looking at umbrellas. She said, "I want the one with the rainbow on it; I like rainbows." I found myself saying, "Well, how about the one with the pretty butterflies instead." What was wrong with her admiring God's beauty and me trying to shy away from it? What was wrong with that picture? Sadly, once again, the world had taken something that God meant for good and turned it into a symbol for a lifestyle that is in direct opposition with what He commands.

Unfortunately, there are many young people, in and outside of the church, who are struggling with and experimenting with same sex relationships. As a teacher, I have seen the phenomenon grow by leaps and bounds as we have watched the family structure rapidly deteriorate.

God keeps His promises!

If you are a young person who has found themselves being caught up in this lifestyle, I want you to know that God can and will deliver you from this. It has never been His will for anyone to perish, but for all to come to repentance (2 Peter 3:9). I was always like the military – don't ask, don't tell. I did not feel comfortable talking about the subject. As a matter of fact, I would pray that I never had to deal with any young people in that situation. Of course, God probably thought I was crazy for making that request. What He did was allow me to be educated about the subject so that I could offer hope and encouragement to young people who found themselves in that situation and wanting to experience God's redemption and grace. There are several reasons I have found why people get trapped in this lifestyle. In the case of Tee, let me tell the rest of her story. One day she was walking around the room (instead of participating in class) and we were having a discussion on child abuse. For once she stopped, stood and listened. I asked her if there was a problem and she said, "This is interesting; this is what happened to me." I immediately had to repent because I had passed judgment on her. This gave her an opening to share some things that she had not shared with anyone. Our relationship grew after that. I found out that her parents were Christians, so I felt comfortable sharing with her from a Godly standpoint. She shared that she had been a victim of sexual abuse when she was younger, and this is why she did not feel comfortable around males. I was able to share with her that God promised to give her back those years that were taken from her. I was also able to refer her for counseling. She said that she wanted me to pray for her. She asked me one day, "Do you think I can ever be normal?" Can you imagine how I felt? Here was this girl, very hard, very angry with the world, and she had been able to break through her shell in front of the whole class. Without question I told her that God can do ANYTHING! There is nothing too hard for God. God may use counselors and others to help people recover from any number of situations, but God is certainly able and willing. Sadly, many young people who were sexually abused as children struggle with their identities and their self-worth. It is so tragic that even a single abuse episode can leave a child scarred for life. Often these children have trouble and turn to all kinds of sexual immorality, including promiscuity, pornography and even homosexuality. It takes a sick person to hurt a child, but as long as sin is in the world- anything can happen. The consolation we have is that God is a healer and will always be there when we call.

I've known young people who were "told" that they were gay because of how they carried themselves. A young man was telling his friends how this guy had hit on him. One said, "But you're not gay." He responded, "I might as well be because people think I am anyway." I felt so bad when I `heard this. Yes, he had some characteristics that appeared feminine, but that did not make him a homosexual. We must remember that words have power. The Bible says that "life and death are in the power of the tongue." But just as other's words have power; your words also have power. You can speak life and triumph over your own self!

Elena was dealing with the loss of her mother. She was being raised by her father and her stepmother. She never said anything bad about either of them. She was well taken care of, but she said that she had never gotten over her mother's death and that put her in a very vulnerable state. She was targeted by one of the most aggressive girls in the school and was pulled into what would be a very tumultuous relationship. Jay was obviously a very troubled girl. She had decided to make it her business to try to get as many "girlfriends" as she could. Daily there were fights in the school because the "girlfriends" were jealous of each other. Elena was involved in many of the fights and arguments, while Jay thought it was funny. I couldn't understand why Elena would want to be involved with anyone that didn't care about her feelings. After the summer after she had her baby, she came back to school and said that she and the father had gotten back together. I did ask her about her other relationship, and she said that was over for good.

One of the common factors involved in many of these situations is hurt. It seems as though young people don't know how to deal with hurt, so they allow themselves to be opened up to a lot of remedies that are not Godly. Sadly, this is true, even in the church.

Some young people who have adopted this lifestyle have not been victims of abuse, but just have been tricked by Satan. Many women, especially in the urban community have become bitter by the consequences of some of the choices they have made in life. They pass along the idea to their girls that "we don't need men." Maybe your feelings have been hurt in the past; maybe you can't find a boyfriend or husband; maybe your boyfriend cheated on you or maybe TV has glamorized this "alternative" lifestyle. Again, don't be tricked into counterfeit love – the only way to lasting peace and contentment is by being obedient to God. One reason why it may be hard to sort this situation out is that everyone inside the church can't seem to agree on whether homosexuality is, in fact, sin. There are some who always want to point out that people are born oriented towards homosexuality, and therefore, it must be okay. That may be so. This is why the Bible says that we must be born again. Along with homosexuality is the transgender trend. This is the belief that God has made a mistake and we can/must correct it. We know that God does not make mistakes. Period. It is important to understand that when Adam and Eve sinned, sin became a permanent part of our existence. Psalm 51:5 says, *"For I was born a sinner – yes, from the moment my mother conceived me."* At birth, we are wired to go in any direction. Our base urges go against God which is why He had to establish rules. There are people born genetically disposed to alcoholism, but still that person can never become an alcoholic if they never drink. Homosexuality is the same way; if you never practice homosexuality, then you cannot be a homosexual. God allows us to make choices about how we are to live our lives. We can choose to live holy or not. To live holy in an unholy world may seem difficult. Paul said that he had to "die daily" which means he had to make a conscious choice every day that he was going to live holy. We need to do the same thing. Going to church on Sunday morning and then just doing whatever during the rest of the week is not going to build you up as a Christian. Another problem that exists for the church is that they don't want to address the problem because they don't know what to say or how to approach the subject. To address the concern about whether it is a sin, the Bible has this to say about homosexuality:

God put a limit on sex. Yes, *a* limit – only one. There is no long discussion on the "do's and don'ts" of sex. The only rule to the enjoyment of sex is this: sex is meant to be enjoyed in the context of marriage – not outside of it. Unfortunately, these days we must be specific. Sex is to be enjoyed within the context of a marriage between a man and a woman. That's it! That's the limit. Genesis 2:24-25 says, *"This explains why a man leaves his father and mother and is joined to his wife, and the two are united into one. Now the man and his wife were both naked, but they felt no shame."* Hebrews 13:4 says, *"Honor marriage, and guard the sacredness of sexual intimacy between wife and husband. God draws a firm line against casual and illicit sex"* (MSG). All sexual sins (for instance promiscuity, adultery,

93

homosexuality, prostitution, etc.) are sins because they do not conform to the limit of sex being a *marital* activity as God defines marriage.

Some people will try to argue that homosexuality is natural and for an argument say that there are gay animals. However, it's not hard to figure out that homosexuality is decidedly *un*natural. God made men and women different, both emotionally and physically. Physically, we were created to fit together anatomically much like a puzzle. Our parts just match up! Like with magnets, they are polarized so that opposites are drawn together. The homosexual is trying to force two like pieces together in blatant disregard for God's natural design! He gave us sex, and the single rule for its use. To use sex for a purpose outside of God's plan is unnatural, and a perversion.

Okay, so you're still not convinced. As a matter of fact, your friend has a gay pastor, the minister of music at the biggest church in town is gay, your Auntie left her husband for her friend Sheila so it must not be wrong. *Leviticus 18:22, and 20:13 both describe homosexuality as "an abomination." Romans 1:26-27 (TM) is very specific when Paul says, "Worse followed. Refusing to know God, they soon didn't know how to be human either—women didn't know how to be women, men didn't know how to be men. Sexually confused, they abused and defiled one another, women with women, men with men—all lust, no love. And then they paid for it, oh, how they paid for it—emptied of God and love, godless and loveless wretches."* There it is, in black and white! Yeah, God said it. So now that we know that homosexuality is a sin, we have to face the fact that we live in an increasingly pro-homosexual society. By looking at the media you would think that almost half the population was gay, when in all actuality, only about 5% of the population is. Almost every TV show or movie has a gay character. The media and the schools heavily promote this lifestyle and are working hard to marginalize those who take a moral, biblical stance on the issue. This has caused some people, even Christians, to display their feelings by becoming violent towards homosexuals and lesbians. Hate is never the answer to anything. Every one of us is sinful, yet every one of us is loved by God. Jesus does not celebrate the attacks on homosexual individuals, and neither should we. "Hate the sin, but love the sinner," is how the saying goes, and that applies to homosexuals as well. God's grace covers us all.

If you are a Christian, you must always be ready to stand up against sin. The word on the street is that you all, the Gen-Z's believe that how people choose to live their lives is acceptable and that older folks are too judgmental. As a Christian, that is a very dangerous position to take. It is the responsibility of the Christian to share the gospel, to keep people out of hell. We live in a society where God is constantly being pushed out. As a result, immorality is prevalent, crime is increasing at unbelievable rates, depression and suicide are at alarming numbers among other things. Some people think that the pandemic of COVID-19 was a result of God being fed-up and showing himself in the earth. What we do know is that nothing happens unless God allows it. During the COVID pandemic the facts are that everything the world worships was shut down. I do believe that God used that opportunity to speak to the hearts and minds of people. I hope that He spoke to you and confirmed to you that He is real, His word is real, and He is in control. We cannot be silent anymore.

So, what steps can a person take to get their life turned around? First, confess to God your sin. I John 1:8-9 says, *"If we claim we have no sin, we are only fooling ourselves and not living in the truth. But if we confess our sins to him, He is faithful and just to forgive us our sins and to cleanse us from all wickedness."* Secondly, know that there are resources to help you. There are Christian organizations that will help you find healing through the power of Jesus Christ. You can find confidential Christian counseling services, books, videos, testimonies and other resources. In some cities there are confidential support groups available. Third, get an accountability partner. This should be someone who will not criticize you, but rather someone who will be a support person to help you with your battle. (Yes, it is a battle!) It is important that you seek out help from other Christians. Some secular counselors emphasize accepting who you are and will not support the Biblical concept that homosexuality is sin, and that Jesus is able and mighty to save. Fourth, forgive yourself, and if you were a victim of abuse, forgive the abuser. I know that this may seem like a difficult thing to do. It doesn't mean that you must actually face the perpetrator, but in order to release yourself for healing you must release the hurt by offering forgiveness to the person that violated you. You can write them a letter and then shred it. You can, in your confession to God, offer a prayer of forgiveness. The old Sunday School song still holds true, "What a friend we have in Jesus, all our sins and grieves to bear, what a privilege to carry everything to God in prayer; O what peace we often forfeit, oh what needless pain we bear, all because we do not carry, everything to God in prayer." *"But you belong to God, my dear children. You have already won a victory over those people, because the Spirit who lives in you is greater than the spirit who lives in the world"* (I John 4:4). Finally, if you are a part of a church where they don't share the Biblical stand against homosexuality, then you need to find a new church. If you are a member of a church where they only speak hatred and not love and redemption for the sinner, you need to find a new church. If you a member of a church and you just think they don't know what to do or how to approach the issue, send the pastor a copy of this book with a note attached. Finally, get into the word, daily, and stay prayed up! When you choose to take a stand against sin, the devil is going to be even more on your case than before. Find a youth group or bible study to join. Don't think that it's going to be smooth sailing because anytime we make the devil mad, he goes on a rampage. There is a song called *Never Be Defeated* by Rich Tolbert, Jr. Listen to it, and be encouraged because we know that the devil has already been defeated, so go on, walk in victory!

Prayer for Me

Dear God,
It's me _____.
I thank you because I am fearfully and wonderfully made. There have been times I have felt abandoned, neglected and/or forgotten. I'm asking you to help me to forgive. My parents might not even know I've felt that way, so please open up the door so I can talk to them. Prepare them to hear what I have to say. I really do want to walk in peace and victory. Forgive me for blaming you for the things that happened to me. You promised that you would restore the years. I'm asking you to do that. Help me to move forward. Don't let me carry the pain of childhood into my relationships. Give me the tools to help somebody else. Surround me with Christians that I can trust and talk to. Thank you.

Dear Daughter,

There has been a lot going on in these past couple of months and I wanted to write you this letter to let you know that regardless of what you've done, I LOVE YOU. Many times when we sin we hurt the people who love us the most. We may feel unloved by them because they are the ones who are handing out the consequences. They may be the ones embarrassed by what happened and may respond in a manner that is unloving. To be honest I know what sexual sin can do to you and I don't want it take hold of you like it did me. It cost me more than I was willing to spend, took me further than I wanted to go and kept me longer than I wanted to be kept. It almost destroyed my life. The reason why it didn't destroy me was because I allowed God to work on me in this area of my life. I had to trust His process and stay connect to Him through prayer, by reading His word and by staying connected to my brothas in Christ and the Christ community (church). I know you because you have my DNA in you. You and I are one of a kind. Whether you realize it or not, I had (God has delivered me over time) some of the same sinful desires you have and have even acted upon them. I'm here to tell you that there is no sin that you can commit that would stop me from loving you or turn my back on you. All have sinned and fallen short of the Glory of God. Sinning just makes you human. God does require for us to respond when we sin and that is to confess it, ask for forgiveness and to repent (turn away from it). Repentance for most is a process but you have to remain faithful to God and His process. When times get tough and the temptation becomes overwhelming, you have to pray, seek His face and never give up. He is faithful and will keep you if you allow Him to. Just remember don't give up on God because He will never give up on you! He's able!! I will continue to pray for you and encourage you towards greatness in Him! Love you always,

-Dad
(written to 17 year old daughter)

Chapter Eight

When My Father and Mother Forsake Me...

Even if my father and mother abandon me, the LORD will hold me close.
(Psalm 27:10)

When I first met Nikki, she was fifteen years old with a 3-year daughter, Brianna. Brianna was conceived after being raped by her young male cousin. Yes, Nikki was only twelve years old when she became a mother. Literally, a baby having a baby. Nikki and Brianna were living with her grandmother's ex-husband and his wife. Nikki not only had to live through a horrific experience, but to add to her struggle, she couldn't even find a home with any of her own family members.

One of my first students was Renita. Renita was bused to the high school first thing in the morning to attend my parenting class. She was the mother of a 2-year-old son. When class was over, she would take the bus back to the middle school where she was a student. Renita's baby was the product of being raped by her stepfather. Thankfully, he was imprisoned. She was very quiet and withdrawn in class, but I tried to show her as much love and acceptance as possible.

Leah was 16 years old when she became pregnant. I have heard many mothers say that if their teen daughter ever got pregnant, they would put her out of the house. This is usually said because they know how disappointed they would be if that ever happened, not that they would really follow through with the threat. However, Leah's mom did just that. She was sent to foster care. You might be thinking "well, her mother did what she said she was going to do." However, in this case, Leah had a 17-year-old sister who was also pregnant at the same time, but she was allowed to stay. Doesn't seem fair, does it? Of course not, especially when you find out the reason. The difference between the two daughters was that Leah, a white girl, was pregnant by an African American boy and her sister was not. That was the only difference!

I realize that each of these stories involve children, yet there are plenty of young people who suffer abandonment, abuse and neglect at the hands of their parents, where no children are involved.

Krissy was a very bright, beautiful young lady; she was academically gifted. She always strived for excellence in her pursuits. Looking only at the outside, one would never know that what she held inside was heart-wrenching. Her mother, a crack abuser who not only neglected her basic needs, but would also, at times, use her daughter as payment for her drug habit.

Finally, Kayla, 17, came to town to live with relatives after being sexually abused by her father. Sadly, this is a situation that we hear about too often. Kayla's case was even more tragic in that her father was the pastor of the church and her mother did not want the church to find out about the abuse and ruin his reputation, so they sent her away.

When Marie came to my teen parenting class, she told me

that she never thought that she could get pregnant. She kept a calendar of all the times that she would have sex, and she literally had sex almost every single day. For that reason, she was not on birth control and felt that she was unable to conceive. As I got to know her, I found out that she had been sexually abused by her uncle when she was younger and that led to her promiscuity.

Babies are special. Children are a blessing, "a heritage from the Lord." I can't think of anything more exciting than the anticipation of the birth of a baby. It's not enough to have elaborate baby showers, but now there are also gender reveal parties. With the benefit of social media, we follow pregnancies in real time with updated baby belly pics. Many hours and dollars are spent decorating the nursery, choosing the right colors and accessories. But just as we pay attention to the details, God is no different. Earlier you were reminded about Psalm 139:13-16 which says *"You made all the delicate inner parts of my body and knit me together in my mother's womb. You watched me as I was being formed in utter seclusion, as I was woven together in the dark of the womb. You saw me before I was born."* That alone should provide comfort to know that God, who made heaven and earth, took particular care to create you. However, if you're feeling abandoned or neglected you might wonder if this was really God's plan from the beginning. You might even wonder or fantasize about what life might have looked like had you been placed in a different womb. Feeling good about yourself might be a far cry from what you really feel. Unfortunately, as we said earlier, we live in a fallen world. When Adam and Eve sinned, God's plan for a perfect world got all out of whack.

Approximately 2.7 million American children have a mother or father in federal or state prison. In the U.S. nearly 400,000 children are living without permanent families in the foster care system. About 100,000 of these children are eligible for adoption, but nearly 32% of these children will wait over three years in foster care before being adopted. Some are never adopted and "age out" of the foster care system.

Across the United States, it is estimated that 7.8 million children are living in homes headed by grandparents or other relatives.

"When my father and my mother forsake me, then the Lord will take me up." Psalm 27:10

Being a teen is tough enough with supportive, loving parents, but when that relationship is shattered it probably seems like the end of the world. Being a parent is one of the most important jobs in the world. Some might argue that is the most important job in the world. God chose parents as the means to bring new life into the world. He gave parents the job of teaching, nurturing, protecting and guiding. It was His design for parents to be mature, compassionate, respectful, loyal, flexible and self-sacrificing. I believe that God's plan called for these tasks to be carried out in a stable place that children could call home. When these things don't happen, children suffer. Sometimes young people suffer because of the choices that their parents make.

Alexandria was a "good girl." She was a smart, kind, and lovable young lady. Her mother was very nice as well but had a history of promiscuity. One day Alexandria confided that she did not feel that she could remain a virgin until marriage, even though she wanted to. When asked why she felt that way, she said that she was so afraid that she would follow in her mother's footsteps. Although it happens a lot, you don't have to make the same poor choices that your parents made. Generational curses can be broken. If you feel that you are in this situation, stop and pray.

Many young people carry bitterness and anger in their hearts because of the void that is created by neglect. When innocence is gone, often with it goes self-confidence, optimism and a trust in people. Many young boys turn to gang violence. Many girls turn to promiscuity. Girls that fall victim to human trafficking are often targeted because they are vulnerable. The average age a teen enters the sex trade in the US is 12 to 14 years old. Many victims are runaway girls who were sexually abused as children. These girls think that they have found the loving home and family they wanted all along, only to soon find themselves performing sex acts in exchange for food, clothing and shelter. You may have heard people say, "If God is such a loving God, why would He allow..." and use this as an excuse to turn their back on God. If this is your situation, please know that God has not forgotten, or abandoned you. Ever since sin entered the world, the devil, who has free reign over the earth, uses whomever he can to do his dirt, and yes, this sometimes means parents. God said that He will be there for us through every situation. Isaiah 41:10 says *"Don't be afraid, for I am with you. Don't be discouraged, for I am your God. I will strengthen you and help you. I will hold you up with my victorious right hand."* You don't have to go on this journey alone. When Jesus began His ministry, He read out of the book of Isaiah where it says, *"The Spirit of the Lord is upon me, because he has anointed me to preach the gospel to the poor; He has sent me to heal the brokenhearted…"* (Luke 4:18-19 KJV). Jesus was saying that He was sent by the Father to heal those broken from emotional trauma and neglect. Jesus is a loving Savior who is willing to hear our prayers, heal our emotional wounds, and fill the voids in our hearts with His presence. If you've grown up without the kind of nurturing that God designed you to have, spend time in prayer and share your hurts with Him. Recognizing our areas of deep need is a first step in overcoming the wounds created by mommy and daddy. Be honest about your pain. Ask Him to teach you to recognize His healing presence and to heal your heart. As you are working through the pain, you may uncover areas of anger that you didn't know were there. One often overlooked category is the girl whose parents are present physically, but sometimes not emotionally. Mothers and fathers that get overly involved in their work or other activities sometimes can unknowingly leave their children feeling neglected. Often, children of pastors feel this way, and because of it, they sometimes turn away from God. Please, please don't let this be you! Sometimes the parents aren't aware of the impact that it has on their children. Most parents think that if their children's physical needs are met, they are doing well in school, and are active in their hobbies, then everything is fine. As a teen, you experience a range of emotions. We adults like to pass it off as "you know she's a teen" or "it must be that time of the month." It's important for you to speak up. Share how you feel. Get your emotional needs met. Don't carry this weight alone.

If you want to move forward, you must learn to forgive

those who have hurt you. Forgiveness is not for them; it is for you. Sometimes the offender may never be repentant or apologetic about what they did. Perhaps, the offender is no longer around or alive. When you hold on to anger and resentment, it will only hinder you, keep you bound to your wounds and give your offender the victory. Unforgiveness eats you up inside. Someone said, "unforgiveness is like you eating rat poisoning but waiting for the rat to die." Forgiveness sets you free. Ask the Lord to help you release your anger and resentment to Him and allow Him to deal with those who have hurt you. Your offender and your wounds will lose their power as you experience the healing power of Christ. Find a trusted adult, perhaps an aunt, grandmother or someone at church who you can talk to. Maybe there is a teacher or counselor at school that you can confide in. It is also important to surround yourself with friends who can be supportive. If you are a Christian, find other Christian friends. Another place to seek help is with a professional Christian counselor. These are people trained to help others in a safe, non-judgmental atmosphere. It is so important to seek help because many girls become vulnerable and sometimes end up in inappropriate intimate relationships, looking for love in all the wrong places. Remember, you are worth more than diamonds and pearls. Like the Oreo cookie; don't give it away. There is no shame is admitting that you need help. You may be saying to yourself, "I'm okay, I don't need help."

As a young lady, your story isn't over yet. As you prepare to move into adulthood, you will want to work through these feelings of abandonment so that you will be emotionally free for the next phase of your life. God can turn your tragedy into triumph, and can you just imagine the testimony that you will have to use for His glory. Remember Kayla, who we met at the beginning of this chapter; well, she recently completed medical school, is doing her residency and is engaged to be married; tragedy into triumph! Krissy is also married, with two children and is working as an RN; tragedy into triumph!

Prayer for Me

Dear God,

It's me _____.

I thank you because I am fearfully and wonderfully made. There have been times I have felt abandoned, neglected and/or forgotten. I'm asking you to help me to forgive. My parents might not even know I've felt that way, so please open up the door so I can talk to them. Prepare them to hear what I have to say. I really do want to walk in peace and victory. Forgive me for blaming you for the things that happened to me. You promised that you would restore the years. I'm asking you to do that. Help me to move forward. Don't let me carry the pain of childhood into my relationships. Give me the tools to help somebody else. Surround me with Christians that I can trust and talk to. Thank you.

Dear Daughters,

I am so blessed to have five very beautiful daughters. You are unique in your personality and abilities. I continue to be amazed by how you are coping with the stresses of marriage, parenting, and employment challenges. I must confess I know I did not affirm you as much as I should have when you were growing up and under my roof. There were times I am sure you would have made different choices if you had received more affirmation from your dad. I hope you find it in your heart to forgive me; as unfortunately, we live forward and learn backward. I have certainly learned much about girls and their emotional needs, but I learned it late. My hope is you will know how much you are loved and appreciated as my daughters and now as friends. I enjoy your company and appreciate you more than you know because of your care, concern and commitment to me and your mother.

I would make one request of you to love God with all your heart and be devoted to your husbands and children. If you put God first, it does mean you will not make mistakes, but it does mean you will always have strength for the journey. Life is hard at times, sometimes very hard, but God's grace is always sufficient for our struggles. I would say to you our God is faithful and, in the end, marriages may fail, and children may disappoint, but God will bring us through. He loves us with an everlasting love, and it is abundant. I love each of you dearly, and I am cheering for you on your journey. Keep the faith and keep on believing and praying because God will answer prayer. Until next time, I remain in your corner and love you truly. Love, Dad

Final Chapter
THE CHALLENGE

Whew! Now that sure was a lot of stuff, packed into this small package. I hope you got the message that sexual purity is what God designed with you in mind. He treasures the marriage relationship so much that He chose to use that analogy to describe the relationship between His son and the church. So how can you prepare yourself for the one that God is preparing for you? You're probably thinking, I'm still a teen, so I'm not getting married for a long time. I want a boyfriend now.

What? After all these horror stories I just told you? But I get it. It's a very natural longing. As humans, we want to feel loved. As children, our parents usually satisfied that need. If we were lucky, we also had aunties, uncles and grandparents that shared in that also. But now as we are becoming independent, moving away from the nest, we want that from outside the home. In our society, there is an obsession with being liked. We live for "likes." Teens, and some adults, obsess over how many "likes" they receive on social media posts. You may be left feeling down when you don't get the amount of "likes" you thought your posts would get or if others instead made negative comments? In many cases, this has led to depression and, in extreme cases, even suicide. How terrible it is that Satan has manipulated our minds so that our emotional health and self-esteem is based on the approval of mostly strangers. So, it is no wonder that if we want to be liked by strangers, we also have the desire to be liked by another real individual. There's nothing wrong with that but we want to make sure that we are "liked" by the right people. Our bodies have changed, and our hormones tell us that it's time for something else. So, let's talk about dating. I want to talk about the 4 W's of Dating: What is dating? Where can we go? What can we do? Who to date?

Before I go on with this, I want you to know that you need to talk to your parent/guardians about what their rules are for dating. I'm going to share what I think are some reasonable guidelines regarding that, but it's their call. Now if their rules are more permissive than mine, then you should come back and follow these, lol!

Let's jump right in here.

WHAT IS DATING?

Dating is simply that time when two people are attracted to each other, they spend time together socially so they can get to know each other to see if they are compatible for perhaps a committed relationship with the possibility of future marriage. For teens, dating should involve group outings, but only with people that your parents know and trust. Sometimes, even in group situations, people are pressured to make decisions to go along with the crowd. So, it's not enough to say, "I'm going out with my friends" or "me and Jackson are going to his cousin's party." For your protection, your parents need to know and approve who you are going to be with. If you are 16 or 17 and your parents think that you are mature enough, you might be allowed to go on a one-on-one date. Now that's only if your parents also know and believe that your date is mature and responsible enough, and they trust you both. By this time, you should be able to determine his trustworthiness. Beware of wolves in sheep's clothing. That is often what causes date-rape cases. There are advantages to dating the guy that you grew up with.

WHERE CAN WE GO?

There are plenty of fun things to do in either groups or one-on-one. I'm just going to give a few suggestions, but the key is knowing yourself and your interests and that can guide you. Before I start the list, I want to say that "Netflix and Chill" is not an appropriate dating activity. Also, alcohol and anything illegal is completely out of the question! Now here is a list and you can add to it.

- School events
- Festivals and carnivals
- Visiting the zoo
- Museums
- Picnics
- Building something together
- Volunteering at local food banks, soup kitchens, and shelters
- Bowling
- Skating
- Making music videos together
- Sledding
- Swimming
- Exercising in a public gym

- Paddle boats or other water-based sports
- Picking fruit at a local fruit farm
- Going to a corn maze
- Dancing game nights (Just Dance or any YouTube video)
- Prepare new recipes
- Watch TED talks or other videos of interest and discuss
- At Christmastime
  o Build gingerbread houses
  o Bake Christmas cookies
  o Build a snowman
  o Go caroling
- Host a theme dinner and movie night
- Bonfire and make s'mores

This is just a very short list of ideas. I want you to think outside the box of just going to the movies or to the local restaurant. If you run out of ideas, there are so many great ones you can find online.

WHAT CAN WE DO?

The list that you just read answers most of the question of "what can we do?" However, if you're looking for physical boundaries, I can help you out with that also. One of the reasons that I strongly suggest delaying one-on-one dating until later is because it often leads down a path that many girls regret traveling. Guys, in and out of the church, feel that sex should be a part of their relationships. Sex absolutely should NOT be a part of your relationship. You must make sure that you avoid getting yourself into compromising situations. My uncle used to say, "If you don't want to die in New York, don't go to New York." In other words, you can avoid uncomfortable situations if you don't put yourselves in them. You should never be alone with a guy in your house, in his house or even your friend's home. If adults are not home, stay out. You should not have guys in your bedroom. I know some parents allow it, but they shouldn't. I want to remind you about the runaway lane - if you don't get started, you won't have to look for an escape plan. Your boundaries have to be firmly established and communicated ahead of time. If your boundaries keep moving back, then it's only a matter of time before there are no boundaries. Beware of "church" guys who say that they are saved "from the waist up." There's no such thing. I Corinthians 6:18 tells us to *"Run from sexual sin! No other sin so clearly affects the body as this one does. For sexual immorality is a sin against your own body."* When you say no sex, that includes other sexual activity, including oral sex, him touching your breasts or vaginal area and you touching his penis. Just don't do it. If that isn't clear, then I can't help you!

WHERE CAN I FIND SOMEONE TO DATE?

What is the best way to find someone to date? You have probably heard that the Bible in Proverbs 18:22 says, "He who finds a wife, finds a good thing." Yes, I know that's what it says. However, there are some practical things that you can do to position yourself to be found. Although you are not currently looking for a husband, you also should not be spending time with guys that are not husband material. By that I mean, even when you are just wanting someone to hang out with, he should still share your morals and values. The best relationships come from people that have shared interests. Church is a great place. It should actually be the best place, but don't be misled; just because a person goes to church doesn't make them a Christian or that they share your same values. So again, the best relationships develop with people that have shared interests. If you are musical, it would be logical that you would attract someone who is also musical. The same concept would apply for athletics, art, or any other special interest. If your school has clubs, join the ones that interest you. This makes sense because you're generally free to be yourself when you are doing things you love, and then you are around people that you have things in common with. The key to attractiveness is not always found in your physical looks, but also in your personality. As teens, we tend to put most of the emphasis on how we look. Don't get me wrong; how you look is important. It is important to make sure that your hair is kept combed, your clothes are neat and clean, and you always smell fresh. I know we all have bad days every now and then, but your bad days shouldn't outnumber your good days. You should always care about your appearance. Having healthy habits is also important. Eating right and keeping your weight under control contributes to your overall appearance. Wearing make-up is something that girls often do, thinking that it will enhance their looks. In some instances, it does, but when it is overdone, it loses its effectiveness. Most guys that I talk to say that they prefer girls that look more natural. Light make-up is okay, but the windshield wiper lashes, and the fuzzy lashes aren't what's going to attract them. The key to attractiveness is confidence. When we are doing what we love and feel good, we carry ourselves in a way that resonates. I had a friend whom some people would see as facially unattractive. But she dripped with confidence. She carried herself extremely well, dressed very nice, was fun to be around and therefore, guys found her irresistible. On the opposite end, Kim was a young lady who had been in an accident when she was younger, so she had sustained a noticeable scar. She was very self-conscious about it and therefore she felt that guys would not find her attractive. She was pretty, smart and had a great personality, however, her low self-esteem opened her up to be used by guys, one in particular. She gave him money to buy drugs; she brought him bags of snacks and food every day. He threatened to stop liking her if she didn't give in to his demands, the Oreo cookie! I tried to talk to her about the situation. She said that she understood what I was telling her, and she would stop, but she found it hard to do. When another young man came along that was attracted to her personality, she couldn't accept the idea that someone liked her for her, so she sabotaged the situation. If you don't love yourself, it is hard for others to do the same. It is also important that your appearance reflect your witness. Don't advertise goods that are not for sale. I heard a church mother say one time: "Don't use your body to get nobody." This can get you in trouble. Earlier we talked about advertising. There is an advertising tactic called bait-and-switch. The store lures you into the store by advertising a "too-good-to-be-true" special. When you get there, they have conveniently run out of the advertised item and try to sell you something else. Don't think that wearing revealing clothes is going to get you the guy that God is preparing for you. As a Christian young lady, you have to be set apart. That doesn't mean wearing long dresses and turtleneck sweaters, but it does mean that you shouldn't wear clothes that show your breasts, your belly and your bottom. I know we exist in this feminist society that says females should be allowed to wear what they want. That's true in a sense, but somehow the attitudes of the world have not changed the DNA of males, and they can be driven by what they see. The Bible reminds us a lot that even though we live in the world, we are not "of" the world. Romans 12:2 states, *"And be not conformed to this world: but be ye transformed by the renewing of your minds, so that ye may prove what is that good, and acceptable, and perfect, will of God"* (KJV). It should be your goal to want to be in the perfect will of God. Now in case you were wondering, I do think that it is okay to text a guy that you like. Believe it or not, guys have some of the same insecurities as you. If he's already a friend, it's okay to send a "how's it going" text or share a funny meme or video. After all, that may show him that you are interested and be the catalyst to get the ball rolling. If he doesn't respond right away, don't feel "some kind of way." It is not the end of the world.

Before I share my final thoughts, I want to share the following letter which was written by my Grandfather, Ezekiel Moore. He had six daughters. It was not known whether this was written for one in particular or for all of them collectively.

A Letter to My Daughter

When the news reached me, while waiting in the corridor of the building where my child was born, the words "Baby Girl Moore," my heart began to build dreams, form sequences, chart courses and devotions in all the highlights of a daughter's life's career.

"Baby Girl," I visualized your smiles, a babe in arms, and longed to hear you coo and sputter words which sounded like things, and "Mama" and "Dada." Your plump little body became a bundle of love and cheer and delight. I loved your growth and development and when in school you learned to read your first books, I recognized some of life's facts. I commenced to live with you, hoping and praying and in a way unknown to youth, living with you.

I saw in you the beauty and charm of your mother again, in your face and in your eyes. Your character reflected her womanhood and her virtue. In your growing years, I began to live anew, in another person, my own daughter, my flesh, my blood, my spirit in a form of feminine charm. I sighed in admiration of you. As you lived, I enjoyed every new thrill and pleasure. I tried so hard to understand you, and yet guide you aright. I loved your laughter and your jest. Though I became firm in my judgments, and lest I see you dear, crumble to embarrassment or disgrace, I ran swiftly to the place, the precipice, where you stood, pondering a decision, seeking only your good. Your wishes became my objectives and my aims. I lost myself in the forests and fields of your desires. My hopes were for your well-being, your happiness. Time, "Baby Girl"

119

brought you to the age when I could no longer make your decisions, nor limit your devotions; neither yet, choose your paths. But my heart traveled on with you. I wondered if you were safe, peaceful and happy after your departure to become another's love, then later, a mother, too.

Life brought you to responsibilities, work, and trials. But I see you still transformed to the smaller years when I called you "Baby Girl." The warm, satisfying memories of you, "Baby Girl," shall ever fill a void reminiscent of those dearest days when you grew up before my eyes—a Father and his daughter.

Daddy

Final Chapter: The Challenge

Finally, don't ever compromise your beliefs, morals and standards just so you can say you got you a "bae." If a guy cannot accept the total you, then he does not deserve you! You are a precious jewel, not an Oreo cookie. You are made in the likeness of God himself. Guard your gift. Trust that God loves you, and He is saving His very best for you. In the meantime, enjoy your youth. Get to know the God that loves you so much that He would have His son die for you. I guarantee that if you get to really know Him, you will really love Him. This will lead you to the most fulfilling relationship ever!

SOURCES

https://www.cdc.gov/healthyyouth/sexualbehaviors/

Posted 5 Sep 2000. Pregnant Pause.org and
http://www.birthmothers.org/extras/types-of-abortions.htm

http://cmc.rodparsley.com/abstinenceeducation.aspx

https://www.cdc.gov/std/stats17/adolescents.htm

https://www.cdc.gov/std/

ABOUT THE AUTHOR

Sandra Dixon, from Cleveland Heights, OH would often tell people that she was the only employee in the school district that had a job because teens were having sex! Go figure, a twenty-something, single young lady from a Holiness Church entrusted with the responsibility of preparing young ladies and men for parenthood. As it turns out, she was the perfect one for the job. She is very passionate about young people. Over the past thirty years, Sandra has taught and mentored young people from all walks of life. The only thing she says that have changed are their names. When not teaching, she can be found working in the church, directing the high school Gospel Choir, traveling, writing plays, crafting, cooking and baking and being a mom to Alexis and wife to Michael James.